O COME, LET US ADORE

O Come,
Let Us Adore

Exploring the Crib at Christmas

Christopher Hayden

VERITAS

Published 2010 by
Veritas Publications
7–8 Lower Abbey Street
Dublin 1, Ireland
publications@veritas.ie
www.veritas.ie

ISBN 978 1 84730 247 2
Copyright © Christopher Hayden, 2010

10 9 8 7 6 5 4 3 2 1

'Epitaph on a Tyrant' by W. H. Auden, from *Poems Selected by John Fuller* (London: Faber and Faber, 2000). 'The Nativity' by G. K. Chesterton, from *Poems by Gilbert K. Chesterton* (New York: Dodd Mead and Co., 1922). 'A Christmas Poem' by Wendy Cope, from *Serious Concerns* (London: Faber and Faber, 2004). 'The Bearer of Evil Tidings' by Robert Frost, from *The Complete Poems of Robert Frost* (New York: Holt, 1949). Excerpt from *Markings* by Dag Hammarskjöld (New York: Ballantine Books/ Epiphany Edition, 1983). 'The Oxen' by Thomas Hardy first appeared in *The Times* (London, 14 December 1915). Excerpt from 'Advent' by Patrick Kavanagh is reprinted from *Collected Poems*, edited by Antoinette Quinn (Allen Lane, 2004), by kind permission of the Trustees of the Estate of the late Katherine B. Kavanagh, through the Jonathan Williams Literary Agency. 'Afar From Where the Sun Doth Rise' translated by R. A. Knox, from *The Divine Office: Volume One* (London: Collins, 1974). Reproduced by kind permission of Continuum International Publishing Group. 'Mass for the Day of St Thomas Didymus' and 'Annunciation' by Denise Levertov, from *New Selected Poems* (Bloodaxe Books, 2003). 'Wir dürfen dich nicht …/We must not portray …' by Rainer Maria Rilke, from *Rilke's Book of Hours: Love Poems to God* translated by Anita Barrows and Joanna Macy, copyright © 1996 by Anita Barrows and Joanna Macy. Used by permission of Riverhead Books, an imprint of Penguin Group (USA) Inc. 'A Christmas Carol' by Christina Rossetti, from T*he Poetical Works of Christina Georgina Rossetti* (London: Macmillan 1904). 'Christmas' by Stevie Smith, from *Collected Poems of Stevie Smith*, copyright © 1972 by Stevie Smith. Reprinted by permission of New Directions Publishing Corp. 'The Nativity' by Henry Vaughan, from *The Poems of Henry Vaughan, Silurist*, Vol II, ed. E. K. Chambers (London: Lawrence and Bullen, 1896). 'Escalator' by Adam Zagajewski, from *Selected Poems* (London: Faber and Faber, 2004).

A catalogue record for this book is available from the British Library.

Designed by Tanya M. Ross

Printed in the Republic of Ireland by Hudson Killeen, Dublin

Veritas books are printed on paper made from the wood pulp of managed forests. For every tree felled, at least one tree is planted, thereby renewing natural resources.

To Tom, Enda, Maeve, Fiona, Ann and Gina

Contents

Chapter One

Setting the Scene: The Real Nature of Things

Christmas Eve, and twelve of the clock.
'Now they are all on their knees,'
An elder said as we sat in a flock
By the embers in heartfelt ease.

We pictured the meek mild creatures where
They dwelt in their strawy pen,
Nor did it occur to one of us there
To doubt they were kneeling then.

So fair a fancy few would weave
In these years! Yet, I feel,
If someone said on Christmas Eve,
'Come; see where the oxen kneel

'In the lonely barton by yonder comb
Our childhood used to know,'
I should go with him in the gloom,
Hoping it might be so.

Thomas Hardy (1840–1928), 'The Oxen'

December 24th, 1915. Christmas Eve. Europe is at war. The trenches of Flanders have been running with blood. Casualties run in the hundreds of thousands. The youth of the nations is being shredded by machine gun fire, suffocated by poisonous gas, reduced to a bloody pulp by shellfire. Gallipoli, Ypres, the Marne – these are among the all-too-familiar names of unthinkable carnage. Innocence is lost in the long night of war, and hope seems hopelessly fragile.

On that date, Christmas Eve 1915, Thomas Hardy's poem, 'The Oxen', appeared in *The Times* of London. Hardy, like many of the literary and intellectual figures of his time, was an unbeliever; he had long abandoned the Christian faith of his earlier life. But on that Christmas Eve, writing as an old man in an immensely dark period of history, Hardy expressed a longing for the reassurance of faith. The focus of his longing was the Christmas story, and the image that drew him was the image of the oxen in the crib. Hardy, like countless others then and since, longed for innocence, but innocence in a dark and broken world seemed no more than 'a fancy few would weave'.

What is it about the crib that evokes such intense nostalgia? What is this strange hold the Christmas story has on the imagination? Is it merely that the story, and the crib which captures it so graphically, fills us with a longing for lost innocence and a lost simplicity? Or could it be that the crib scene resonates with an innocence and a simplicity that we have not lost? Perhaps the crib touches so many people so deeply precisely because it taps into qualities within them that may be largely forgotten, but are not entirely lost. In the 'gloom' so poignantly captured by Hardy's poem, it could be that the crib does not so much weave a spell of compensatory fantasy, as remind us of the real nature of things.

The real nature of things. This will be the starting point for these reflections: the conviction that the crib, far from inviting a flight from the harshness of reality, speaks of and to reality. Of course, the crib can be a vehicle for saccharine sentimentality, for a kind of soft emotionalism posing as religion; the crib can appear to provide a justification for the notion that religion is – largely if not exclusively – for children. But this need not and should not be so. The crib is not a sweet but inconsequential collection of toys. It actually represents a reality that has the potential to change lives and societies. The early Christians discovered this quickly, as did their opponents, who feared the change that had been heralded by the coming of Christ. In fact, the earliest opponents of Christianity may have understood better than the Christians themselves that, far from inviting complacency or passivity, the Christmas story shatters complacency and invites active engagement. While the modern despisers of Christianity may resort to scorn and ridicule, their earliest forbears feared the enormous potential that had been unleashed at the first Christmas. It was this fear that motivated those who sought to stamp out its potential. Herod, as we shall see, tried to do so at Christ's birth, in an act of indiscriminate slaughter. The chief priests tried to do so after Christ's resurrection, by spreading the rumour that he had not risen from the tomb, but that his body had been stolen. If the enemies of the Gospel could take Christ so seriously, it behoves those who would claim to be his friends to do no less.

It begins to become clear that the crib, which captures the beginnings of Christ and the beginnings of Christianity, has a certain paradoxical quality. On the one hand, it evokes tremendous nostalgia, the kind of nostalgia that inspired Hardy's wartime poem; the kind that continues to instil a mood of sad longing in many people each Christmas. On the other hand, properly understood, the crib is a call to action, to a new and fresh way of thinking and of living. Heaping paradox upon paradox, we could say that the real reveille is sounded not by a soldier's trumpet in a wartime barracks, but by the angelic trumpet heralding the birth of the Prince of Peace. The trumpet sounds, not for war, but for peace, yet it is also a call to arms. A few decades after Christ's birth, Saint Paul would write that these arms include truth, righteousness, faith, and confidence in the promise of salvation.

How should we approach this paradox of the crib, so that it might both touch our emotions and impact on our lives? Without doubt, we should affirm, rather than shy away from, the wonderful emotional appeal of the crib. The Christmas scene truly is, in the broadest sense of the word, magical. We do no disservice to a robustly adult faith by allowing ourselves to be charmed, touched, and romanced by the crib. If the crib fills us with nostalgia, if it moves us, we can accept this with gratitude, mindful that the noblest actions result from individuals being moved to act. In the poem 'Advent', Patrick Kavanagh writes that the point of Advent preparation is to 'charm back the luxury / Of a child's soul'. The innocence of a child's soul is indeed a precious possession, one that adults have generally lost, at least in part. But if it is a luxury, it is not an expensive one, and it can be charmed back by the simplicity of the crib. The emotional appeal of the crib can find a chink in our all-too-adult armour, a place where the full message of Christ can begin to enter, and set about its steady work of transformation.

What Kavanagh describes as charming back the luxury of a child's soul, has much in common with the thinking of some religious scholars, who have described this as 're-enchantment'. Individuals can, of course, be disenchanted by the disappointments, tragedies and hardships of life; but in many ways the world itself has become disenchanted. With science offering ready explanations and technology offering limitless, instant information, there seems to be less room for mystery, for a sense of wonder and enchantment around the unexplained edges of things. Some people insist that this is the way it should be, that the disenchantment of the world is part of the coming of age of humanity, that religion and mystery are being left behind by technical progress and scientific understanding. But this insistence does not take account of the virtually limitless human thirst for the transcendent, which can be seen in an explosion of all kinds of spiritual interests in our time. The more rigorous proponents of a strictly scientific view of the universe may look on askance, but today, the human spirit is doing its own thing, dancing its own dance. Countless groups and individuals are reaching out, at times in undisciplined or unenlightened ways, seeking and demanding the re-enchantment of the world.

The crib can re-enchant: it can draw us back into the mystery of God. Far from fostering a flight from the world and its concerns, such re-enchantment leads us straight to the heart of reality. In the story captured by the crib, we find good and evil, acceptance and rejection, love and hatred, darkness and light. This is the stuff of real life, not of escapist fantasy.

But just how real is the crib itself? It is worth dwelling on this question for a moment, since there is a certain kind of austere biblical scholarship that would consider the crib to be merely an object of devotion, and one that does not take sufficient account of the nature of the Gospel stories. The crib includes characters from two of the four Gospels; it places Matthew's magi alongside Luke's shepherds; it includes Matthew's star and Luke's angel. Of course the crib would not be complete without the humble ox and ass, and a meek lamb draped over a shepherd's shoulders, and yet these creatures are not mentioned in the Gospels at all. We could say that the crib combines different casts of characters, but without taking account of the different – and separately written – dramas in which the characters were originally involved. To use a word beloved of biblical scholars, the crib 'conflates' different accounts: it blithely mixes and mingles, drawing together two originally separate versions of the story of Jesus' birth, but without attaching any particular significance to the distinctive origins of each story.

From the point of view of academic biblical scholarship, this could indeed be considered a mistake. Matthew and Luke each tell the story of Jesus' birth in their own way and for different audiences. Luke writes his Gospel for a rather poor community. Unlike Matthew, Luke takes care to note the poor circumstances in which Jesus spent the earliest hours of his life: he was placed in a rough feeding trough – a manger. Furthermore, the only visitors Luke mentions are poor shepherds. Matthew writes to a better-off community: he makes no reference to the circumstances of Jesus' birth, and he does not fear making his readers feel excluded by his mention of some obviously wealthy visitors – the Magi, who had been able to afford a long trip, and who had brought expensive gifts for the newborn child.

We shall reflect further on the differences between Matthew and Luke when we come to consider the visit of the wise men. For now, suffice it to say that the tradition of the crib is greatly enriched by the fact that the Gospels give not one, but two accounts of the birth of Jesus. And the fact that the crib combines them does not diminish this enrichment. The crib scene does not impoverish our understanding: it enriches our imagination. It is replete with all the richness of the Gospels – a feast for the eye, the heart and the mind. It is not an academic commentary on a set of Gospel passages, but a vivid and faithful presentation of the coming of the Saviour. The kind of academic austerity that would caution against forgetting the particular concerns of Luke and Matthew need not concern us unduly, yet we will take care to keep our reflections grounded in solid scholarship. Scholarship is a blessing to believers: in allowing ourselves to be guided by its insights and its concern for historical detail, we guard against letting the priceless gift of imagination degenerate into fantasy.

The crib is not as old as the story it tells. Some depictions of the story of Christ's birth date back to the early centuries, and the ox and ass already figure in a Roman carving from the middle of the fourth century. It was Saint Francis of Assisi who pioneered the crib as a popular devotion. In 1223, using live characters, he created a crib that captured people's imagination, and the custom of setting up cribs began to spread. It is worthwhile to recall that in the time of Saint Francis, the vast majority of people – though not Francis himself – were illiterate. Rather like the ancient Irish high crosses, which were often covered with engravings of biblical scenes, the crib was a text that everyone could read.

Illiteracy is, of course, no blessing. Yet in the case of the crib, illiteracy proved to be a cloud with a silver lining. Like illiteracy, propaganda is a negative-sounding reality, but – again like illiteracy – it has a certain serendipitous connection with the crib. Luke begins his Christmas story with a mention of Caesar Augustus, the first Roman emperor. Augustus was a brilliant military leader; he had brought an end to decades of civil war, and by the time of Jesus' birth, he was being revered as a bringer of peace, the lord and saviour of his people. But the peace brought by Augustus did not come about through reconciliation between enemies – it was a peace brought by the sword, by the utter and merciless defeat of the enemies of Rome. Political propaganda is no modern invention; the reign of Augustus was buttressed by widespread propaganda. One particularly striking example of such propaganda read as follows: 'The birthday of the god was the beginning of the good tidings for the world.' These words, found on an inscription commemorating the birthday of Caesar Augustus, date from the year 9 BC, yet they sound tailor-made for the birth of Christ. The angel in Luke's Gospel proclaims to the shepherds the birth of a Saviour, who is Christ, the Lord, while the heavenly host proclaims peace on earth.

The similarity between the birthday acclamation for Caesar Augustus and the annunciation of the birthday of Jesus is not accidental. Luke the evangelist is deliberately hijacking the language of imperial propaganda; he is indulging in counter-propaganda of the most blatant kind. To spell out the message of Luke's counter-propaganda is not difficult: Yes! The Saviour has been born. No! It is not Caesar. Yes! The bringer of peace is among us. No! It is not Caesar. Yes! God is in our midst. But no! Not in the person of Caesar. As for the crib, it continues this none-too-subtle propaganda, applying it to our own time and our own lives: in the newborn child, our God is here, among us bringing peace. But God is at work in hiddenness, in littleness, in poor and humble circumstances. We need not look to greatness, wealth, triumph or power. While we may hope for progress in politics, we need not expect any worldly power to deliver definitive justice or peace. There is no utopia waiting to be ushered in by coercion or by some paradigm shift in human attitudes. Rather there is, the angel tells us and the crib reminds us, God's own offer of peace on earth to people of goodwill. In the face of the glittering promises and propaganda of this world, the crib gently and insistently proclaims God's own counter-propaganda.

We have mentioned that staying grounded in solid historical scholarship helps to keep our imagination from running out of control. Imagination is, as we noted, a priceless gift; unchecked, it has the potential to lead us astray, but without it, our faith might consist of little more than a series of abstractions. At the very least, religion devoid of imagination lacks texture, depth and colour. The crib both taps into and invites religious imagination. In the most positive sense of the expression, we can say that the crib is a perfect target for pious embellishment. How many people, for example, imagine Jesus to have been born on a sultry, rainy afternoon? He was born, the imaginative words of a Christmas carol tell us, 'on a cold winter's night that was so deep'. Obviously, we know nothing about the weather conditions, but another carol assumes that on the night of Christ's birth the wind was not blowing: 'O little town of Bethlehem, how still we see thee lie!' These small details of pious embellishment carry their own truth. They capture the insight that the world into which the Saviour was born was dark and becalmed: a world that was stuck, motionless, a world without light. The one born into that dark stillness would grow up to proclaim: 'I am the light of the world.' And while he would calm a storm on the Sea of Galilee, he would also bring about the mighty, world-changing wind of Pentecost.

We might think as well of the innkeeper, earnest supporting actor in countless children's nativity plays. He is not mentioned in the Gospel story, which merely tells us that there was no room at the inn. Nor, for that matter, does the innkeeper figure in the crib. Yet he figures prominently in the Christian imagination. It is he who acts out that part in each of us that would, at least from time to time, say to the Lord, 'Go away, I have no room for you'. Popular imagination and its offspring, pious embellishment, can be excellent teachers. While we may need to approach them with a degree of reserve, we may do well to heed what they have to say.

Illiteracy, propaganda and pious embellishment are at first glance perhaps not the most auspicious of concepts, yet they have attributed to the emergence of the crib as a significant emblem of Catholic faith. These terms have begun to set the stage, to convey the fact that God does not work according to the established canons of human efficiency. We can also bear in mind the pastoral initiative of Saint Francis of Assisi, the wartime nostalgia of a brilliant but unbelieving poet, the determined protestations of diminutive inn-keepers in school nativity plays. All of these, combined with the details of Roman history and the Gospel accounts of Christ's birth, invite us to take a fresh look at the nativity scene. Sentiment and imagination find a ready welcome at the crib, but only to be refined there, as they encounter the reality of what God was doing and continues to do in the person of Christ the Saviour.

Points to ponder

✝ The Gospel of Luke offers a suggestive insight into the attitude of Mary the mother of Jesus. Luke tells us that when the visiting shepherds had told their story, everyone who heard them was struck with wonder. Mary, however, seems to have taken a more measured and reflective approach: the Gospel tells us that she 'held on to' or 'kept' all the details she had heard, and 'pondered them in her heart'. Mary was not swept along by the immediacy and intensity of the general reaction to the angels' announcement. She intuited that there was more happening than could be understood straight away, or processed in a moment of enthusiasm. As we reflect on the crib, we will be guided by Mary's example: at the end of each reflection we will offer some thoughts for further reflection. These thoughts will be offered as a way of holding onto and pondering some of what we have seen. At the end of each chapter, the final thought will include an invitation to ponder a passage of scripture that may further illuminate our reflections.

+ Every year, many believers feel something more than simple nostalgia: they feel excluded from the spirit of Christmas by loss, depression, or other suffering. Without doubt, there is a superficial, hyped-up way of celebrating Christmas that can exacerbate the sense of exclusion felt by the most vulnerable. We would do well to reflect on how we might pursue a more thoughtful and authentic way of celebrating – one that might make it clear that Christmas is most relevant to those who are in darkness.

+ Our Christian faith has a solid intellectual core, yet there is very much more to faith than a list of doctrinal truths. At the centre of our faith is a person: Christ himself. Imagination and emotion need no more be a hindrance to a relationship with Christ than they are to any other relationship; in fact, imagination and emotion can provide enrichment to our spirituality. Hopefully, our contemplation of the crib in the pages that follow will help to lead us to a faith that is more heartfelt, a faith that has caught fire, a faith that does not simply know the truth of Christ, but is touched and enchanted by that truth.

+ In the prophet Isaiah (55:8-9) we read: 'For my thoughts are not your thoughts, neither are your ways my ways, says the Lord. For as the heavens are higher than the earth, so are my ways higher than your ways and my thoughts higher than your thoughts.' By God's providence, the combination of illiteracy, propaganda and pious embellishment proves to be, not an obstacle, but a powerful vehicle of grace. The crib invites us to reflect on areas in our own lives where God may be acting in ways that are hidden or surprising, in ways that seem contrary to human wisdom.

Chapter Two

To Bethlehem: Caesar and his Census

> O come, all ye faithful,
> Joyful and triumphant,
> O come ye, O come ye to Bethlehem;
> Come and behold him
> Born the King of Angels.
> O come, let us adore him ...
>
> John Francis Wade (1711–1786)

Of the four evangelists, Luke is the keenest historian. He carefully names the leaders of his day: emperors, governors and kings. But they are merely the backdrop to the real story, the one planned by God's providence and now unfolding in Jesus. While God works in and through history, he does not do so in a way that historians can detect. The history Luke recounts is real history, but history is simply not big enough to contain the full meaning of events that are taking place, and will continue to take place in Jesus. Before considering Luke's grand historical picture, let us reflect for a moment on the fact that some truths are bigger than history.

About six decades after the birth of Jesus, Saint Paul, writing to Christians in the Greek city of Corinth, stated very simply: 'Christ died for our sins' (1 Cor 15:3). We can divide this short statement into two parts: one that is a statement of history, the other that conveys more than any historical statement can. The words 'Christ died' plainly convey the fact that a particular person, known as the Christ, died. Christ, the Messiah, did not live forever; at a particular moment his life ended. The fact of Christ's death was observable – even by those who did not regard him as the Christ. At the very least, people who witnessed the crucifixion could see that a person acclaimed as the Christ had died. This observable fact was passed on, and eventually written down as a plain fact of history.

What about the words 'for our sins'? The assertion that Christ died for our sins doesn't merely provide information about his death. It conveys something that is beyond the view of history, something accessible only to faith. Nobody on Calvary – disciple, soldier or curious bystander – could see that this person was dying 'for our sins'. This was not a plain, observable fact. It was an understanding that grew in the hearts and minds of Jesus' followers, as they reflected, with the light of the Holy Spirit, on what they had seen and heard.

The faith understanding that Christ not only died, but died for our sins, does not contradict any fact of history: rather, it expresses a reality that no historian can fully describe. The utterly real fact that Christ died for our sins is outside of history, in the very sense that God himself is. God works in and through all events, but God's control of events stems from the fact that he is not controlled by them. There is more to this than pure historical description can contain or convey. This is the case at the end of Christ's life; it also the case at the beginning.

For Luke the evangelist, the events of the first Christmas are solid, concrete fact. Luke locates these events on a wide political canvas, but his references to prominent figures at the time of Jesus' birth are designed to make it clear that Jesus, not Caesar, is the centre of history. The God who is beyond history has entered it in the person of Jesus, and a large part of Luke's purpose in writing his account is to show that the birth of Jesus has changed history. Bethlehem does not know it yet, nor do Jerusalem or Rome, but the child in the manger is beginning to fulfil the prophecy made by his mother shortly after she conceived him: 'He has brought down the powerful from their thrones, and lifted up the lowly' (Lk 1:52).

Luke begins his telling of the story of Jesus' birth by letting us know who was in charge at the time, and the irony is almost comical. Caesar Augustus is exercising his authority over humanity by demanding a census of the whole world. Quirinius, governor of Syria, Caesar's regional representative, is responsible for that part of the world where Luke's story is unfolding. Joseph, an unimportant individual from a backwater called Nazareth, is complying with the orders of these powerful men. He is coming to Bethlehem to register, along with Mary, to whom he is engaged. Mary, in her turn, is carrying an unborn child, who at this moment in the story is not even referred to by name, and the whole business is conspiring to set the scene for the birth of the Saviour. Who is in charge? God is. Where is the power being exercised? In Caesar's palace in Rome? In the governor's residence in Damascus? No! The power at work is God's own power, and it is being exercised on the outskirts of a small town called Bethlehem, itself just beyond the outskirts of the city of Jerusalem, capital of a troublesome but otherwise insignificant outpost of the mighty Roman empire. All a long way from the corridors of power and the deliberations of the mighty.

One scholar has made the keen observation that the characters mentioned at the beginning of Luke's Christmas story appear in reverse order of importance. First Caesar, great in his own eyes and feared by all. Next his powerful regional representative, Quirinius. Then Joseph, followed by Mary, who is carrying the unborn Son of God. God is indeed acting through the events of history, but he does so by turning things on their head. Some of the earliest opponents of Christianity spoke the unvarnished truth when they alleged that the Christians were a threat to Caesar and had turned the world upside down (Acts 17:6).

How odd it would appear if, on our birth cert, there was a mention that we were born while so-and-so was president of the United States, or while such-and-such a country was applying for membership of the EU. It would, at the very least, seem a tad grandiose. But in setting the stage for Jesus' birth, Luke is not at all shy about including the powers-that-be, because these are the very powers that are to be subverted by the birth of the infant.

And so Joseph, Mary and the unborn Jesus come to Bethlehem. Providence has worked to lead grand events of history to a culmination in this simple, as yet unheralded, arrival. The immediate reason for the trip to Bethlehem was, of course, an exercise in Roman bureaucracy: Joseph, as head of a family-in-the-making, was obliged to respond to the demands of a centralised bureaucratic system. The trip to the Bethlehem census station was neither pilgrimage nor holiday – it was an experience of drudgery. For those who had to travel any distance, every step of the way was a resented reminder that theirs was an occupied country, under foreign control. In this context of foreign political domination, divine providence was doing far more than simply making the best of a bad lot. God was at work in and through the very realities that caused upheaval and bitterness.

In our contemplation of the crib, the trip to Bethlehem – with all its attendant hardships – can make us mindful of a trip on which Joseph would lead his family some twelve years later: the pilgrimage to Jerusalem. Unlike the census journey, the later trip was not an obligation imposed by faceless bureaucrats representing the imperial power, but a grateful and joyful expression of faith. During the annual Passover pilgrimage, the faithful thanked God for delivering them from their captivity to a foreign power. But whereas the trip to Bethlehem was gladdened by the birth of Jesus, the trip to Jerusalem was marred by the three-day ordeal of the parents of Jesus, who were terribly anxious for his whereabouts. The three-day absence of the boy Jesus signalled, far in advance, the three days he would spend in the tomb. We shall see that the crib too contains signals of the sacrificial death that lay ahead of the infant in the manger.

The town of Bethlehem was about five miles south of the centre of Jerusalem. Matthew quotes a biblical prophecy that a ruler of Israel would come from the town; Luke refers to Bethlehem as 'The city of David'. Bethlehem was, in fact, the hometown of David, King of Judah and founder of the monarchy, which became known as the House of David. By letting us know that Jesus was born in Bethlehem, the evangelists are underlining his importance as a great leader. But for now, the greatness of Jesus is hidden. He has been born in obscurity; he is marginal; the child of a temporarily homeless family. The sign in the heavens was discerned only by the wise men; the message of the angels was heard only by a few shepherds. Anyone searching for the trappings of greatness on that night in Bethlehem would have been disappointed.

In the great unfolding story of the birth of the Son of God, the most particular thing about the town of Bethlehem is precisely that it is a particular town, and not an abstract 'everyplace'. God is not a God of philosophical speculation, who brings things to pass in some universal, abstract way. On the contrary, God's workings unfold in particular, concrete ways. People of a slightly philosophical cast of mind sometimes feel offended at the idea that God should choose, should differentiate, between one time and another, one place and another, one people and another. If God really is all-powerful, then why does he not bring things about more directly and more universally, rather than through a slow, hidden and often painful process? Why did God's designs for humanity reach their high point in a particular individual, Jesus, who was a member of a particular nation, Israel, and who was born at a particular time and in a particular place?

We do not fully understand why God chose this given set of details. For his own reasons, God chose to commit what has been referred to as the 'scandal of the particular': in favouring some times, people and places, God seems to have dealt less generously with others. This 'scandal of the particular', however, falls away when we bear in mind the fundamental Christian truth that God blesses people through other people. The prophets of the Old Testament, for example, make it very clear that God chose the people of Israel not so they could glory in having been chosen, but so that ultimately they might be a light to the nations. When God appears to favour particular individuals, or to bless them more generously, it is so that his blessings might spread outwards from them. We can say then that God is indeed a God of particularity, but not a God of exclusiveness. His blessings may appear to follow certain routes, but he intends them to reach everyone. The greatest, most universal and most far-reaching of all God's blessings started life in one particular – we might indeed say peculiar – place: a manger close to the town of Bethlehem.

From the point of view of the Roman Empire, a census was an ambitious affair that had two purposes. It was to let the authorities know how much tax revenue they could expect, and how many men were available for military service (although in fact Jews were generally exempt from military service). It is a great irony that, from another perspective, the census that brought Joseph, Mary and the unborn Jesus to Bethlehem was simply a link in the chain of God's providence.

The idea of census or enrolment finds a mixed reaction in the Bible. A thousand years before the birth of Christ, King David had demanded a census of his people, in order to assess how many men he could press into military service. Here is how one biblical historian describes David's action: 'Satan stood up against Israel, and incited David to count the people of Israel' (1 Chron 21:1). As far as that writer was concerned, David's census exceeded the powers that are proper to a king. Even the King's powers were limited; even the King was subject to a higher power. This was not a concept that the Roman emperors would warm to centuries later. Caesar's power was boundless, and as far as he was concerned, Caesar was himself the higher power. Anyone who would challenge this view would do so at their peril.

Another enrolment, one that is mentioned several times in the Bible, is the enrolment carried out by God. God knows the names of his beloved: they are written in the book of Life (Ps 69:28; Dan 12:1). Especially in times of difficulty, God's faithful people could take comfort from the fact that their names were written on God's roll book. The book of Revelation, which was written to offer hope and consolation to persecuted Christians, repeatedly mentions the grim fate awaiting the persecutors, and all those whose names are not found in the book of Life. Likewise, in the letter to the Philippians (4:3), Saint Paul reminds his readers that their names are recorded in God's book of life, and then immediately breaks into repeated exhortations to rejoice. While the powers of this world carry out censuses in order to take things from those listed on them, God's census is designed only to give and to bless. God's census is a cause of delight, not of resentment. All of this highlights yet another irony in the Christmas story: the census imposed by Caesar proves to be part of the great process of blessing, through which countless people will be enrolled in the book of Life.

Points to ponder

+ The Gospel accounts of the first Christmas make it clear that God is the master of history. The powers of this world come and go, as do their political ambitions and concerns. What abides is the providence of God, which embraces all that happens in this world. Nobody is beyond the reach of providence: even the mighty Caesar, who presumed to exercise authority over the whole world, unwittingly played a part in God's plans to bless the whole world. For us as believers, renewed faith in God's providence working through history is more necessary than ever, in this era of global anxiety.

✤ We have been enrolled, and not only by the census-takers who call to our doors every few years. A great and very concrete sign of our enrolment by God is the baptismal register which contains the details of our baptism. In this large tome we can touch the truth that we are 'on God's books'. God knows us. His Son has told us that every hair on our head has been counted. We might reflect on the significance of some commonplace instances of enrolment. Our address books, for example, or the directories of names in our mobile phones are types of enrolment. There, we find the names of those we love, of those who keep us awake with worry. In these familiar lists, we find not just our contacts, but our heart. Every database, every census and every official record can be a reminder to us that we are known intimately to a loving God, and that our names are carefully recorded on his 'contacts list'.

✤ The circumstances of Christ's birth show us that God acts not at centre stage, but in the wings, on the margins, in smallness and hiddenness. History, including our personal history, is not 'one blessed thing after another', but all things conspiring to bless. Saint Paul was convinced that nothing at all, small or great, hidden or open, could ever thwart God's plans to bless. This confidence of Paul's rested on the realisation that God does not 'get around' obstacles, or work in spite of them. Rather, God's infinite, loving genius – for which we use the term 'providence' – works in and through all things: 'We know that all things work together for good for those who love God, who are called according to his purpose' (Rom 8:28).

Chapter Three

'We have come to worship': The Visit of the Wise Men

> We three kings of Orient are
> Bearing gifts we traverse afar;
> Field and fountain, moor and mountain,
> Following yonder star.
>
> *O star of wonder, star of night*
> *Star with royal beauty bright,*
> *Westward leading, still proceeding,*
> *Guide us to thy perfect light.*
>
> John Henry Hopkins (1820–1891)

Now that we are starting to look at the crib's cast of characters, its *dramatis personae*, why begin with the wise men? They were, after all, the last to arrive. We could, of course, have left them until after Jesus, since they arrived some time after his birth. But the real 'star' of the crib is Jesus himself, and it is quite in order to build up to him by considering some of the other characters first. The wise men, or three kings, appear to have begun their search quite some time before the birth of Jesus, and they probably left their country before Mary and Joseph left Nazareth. The wise men represent the thirst for light, truth and goodness that is in the heart of every man and woman, a thirst that is at the beginning of every religious quest, which is a sufficient reason to begin with the last arrivals.

Who were the wise men? The Greek of Matthew's Gospel calls them *Magoi*, from which we get the English word Magi. These words are close cousins of the words 'magic' and 'magician', and it would be both possible and misleading to refer to these mysterious visitors to the crib as 'magicians'. Possible, given the language of the Gospel and the fact that Matthew probably wants to convey a sense of mystery and intrigue; but misleading, since in common language a magician is someone who plays tricks, and magic is about manipulation and control of hidden powers, rather than the search for God's will. Far from seeking any kind of spiritual control, our visitors from the East are submitting to the pull, the fascination, being exerted on them by God's unfolding plan. Indeed, this is as good a perspective as any from which to view these mysterious individuals: they have felt something of the magnetism of God and his ways; it's not that they understand all that is happening, but they are willing to be led, to discern and follow their deepest intuition and the deepest desires that God has placed in their hearts.

But if the wise men are not magicians, then just who are they and why has Luke included them in his story? As is so often the case, in order to understand this particular Gospel episode, we need to look to the Old Testament, and here it is the book of the prophet Isaiah that comes to our assistance. Isaiah's fundamental conviction is that one day, all the peoples of the earth will turn to God in joyful, trusting faith. That conviction is expressed through the imagery of people travelling to Jerusalem from the ends of the earth. Jerusalem, the holy city, was the place where heaven touched earth. The Jerusalem Temple, located on top of Mount Sion, was the place where God resided. Near the beginning of his book, the prophet Isaiah tells us that at some future time, people from many nations would say: 'Come, let us go up to the mountain of the Lord ... that he may teach us his ways and that we may walk in his paths' (Isa 2:3).

This is just what the wise men are doing; they are making their way to Jerusalem – or at least to a small town on the outskirts of the city. On their arrival – not at the Temple but at a stable – the wise men pay homage, not to a great king, but to a newborn child. The fulfilment of the promises made in Isaiah has now begun, and the wise men are anticipating the procession of nations. For the time being, things will happen in a hidden, humble way, but eventually the glory of God will be visible to all.

But what about the camels? Or should that be dromedaries? It might come as a surprise that the Gospel makes no mention of such creatures. So where do we get the image of tall camels loping towards Jerusalem beneath a starry sky? Once again, the prophet Isaiah provides the necessary background: near the end of the book, as the prophet looks to the future when the whole world will see and respond to the goodness of God, he mentions a 'multitude of camels' that will come with gold and incense (Isa 60:6). The prophet also writes of people coming on dromedaries to the holy mountain, which is Jerusalem (Isa 66:20). While we might well expect dignitaries travelling from the East to have used camels as their means of transport, it is the prophecies of Isaiah that give us the deepest roots of this tradition. From a strictly historical point of view, we know virtually nothing about the wise men, but the scriptures make it clear that in these mysterious figures, God has set in motion his plan to bring all the peoples of the world to his son Jesus.

And then to the star, the heavenly body that the wise men followed from the East, and that eventually settled over the stable at Bethlehem. Biblical scholars with a scientific turn of mind have long speculated whether the star was a supernova, or a comet, or an alignment of planets and stars. Astronomy has been invoked in the attempt to single out a particular comet on a particular date that might fit the bill. But these attempted explanations fall wide of the mark. For one thing, even if the star is to be explained in strictly natural terms, the timing of its appearance would still be miraculous. What's more, neither stars nor comets have the habit of stopping over mangers. The Gospel intends us to understand that even nature is miraculously caught up in the birth of Christ. God is completely and serenely in control of the forces of nature; and nature itself, just as in the case of the star, is a signpost pointing towards the goodness and majesty of God. Some decades later, Saint Paul would write: 'Ever since the creation of the world, his eternal power and divine nature, invisible though they are, have been understood and seen through the things he has made' (Rom 1:20). The child above whom the star came to rest would grow up to say that, at his second coming in glory, people would see not a star stopping in the sky, but stars falling from the sky (Mt 24:29). For the moment, however, the Lord of Glory is but a child, and his presence is marked by a single star seen by but a handful of men.

It has been suggested that the Gospel's mention of the star is a deliberate challenge to astrology and superstition of all kinds: if even the heavenly bodies are now subject to the newborn Christ, then there can be no more room for magical appeal to the forces of nature. All of these forces must now bow down to the one who before long will walk on water, heal the sick, multiply loaves, and calm a storm. In halting, bowing, over the place where Jesus sleeps, the star anticipates the fact that 'at the name of Jesus, every knee should bend, in heaven and on earth and under the earth, and every tongue should confess that Jesus Christ is Lord, to the glory of God the Father' (Phil 2:10-11). On this night, the universe bows to a sleeping infant. Great mysteries have begun to unfold.

Far from being deflated or jaded by their long journey, the wise men were filled with enthusiasm when they saw the star coming to rest over the place where Jesus lay. In one translation of Matthew's Gospel, we read that they were 'overwhelmed' with joy, but a more accurate translation of Matthew's Greek would be: 'They rejoiced exceedingly with great joy.' There is hardly a more joy-filled expression in all the Bible! The only proper response to the newborn in the manger is delight, and the wise men, having reached the end of their journey, feel this delight in abundance.

Their joy at the birth of Jesus and the homage they offer are the finest gifts they can bring, but the wise men also bear gifts of gold, frankincense and myrrh. Incidentally, it is because the Gospel mentions three gifts that tradition has it that there were three wise men, although we are not told this explicitly. Each of the three gifts has its own particular significance. Gold is a gift fit for a king, and on their arrival in Jerusalem, the wise men made it clear that they had come to do homage to the King of the Jews. The next time Jesus will be acclaimed with this title is during his Passion, when Pilate will ask him if he truly is the King of the Jews; when soldiers will use the title mockingly; and when the words 'King of the Jews' will be written on a sign attached to the cross just above Jesus' thorn-crowned head. Nobody present could fully have anticipated these details of the end of Jesus' earthly life, but even now, the circumstances of Jesus' birth hint at what Jesus would say to Pilate during his trial: 'My kingdom is not from this world' (Jn 18:36).

The second gift mentioned is frankincense. An ancient tradition insists that this gift was a recognition of the divinity of Jesus. Incense was, and still today often is used in worship: the rising of incense-smoke symbolises the prayers of worshippers rising to God. Incense would also have been an appropriate gift for a priest, since it was the priest who used it in worship. While we can't be certain that Matthew had these details in mind as he wrote down the story of the wise men's visit, these aspects of the gift of frankincense make it an appropriate and very telling gift for Jesus, the newborn who is 'God from God', and who in his human nature will act as high priest, reconciling all people to God.

We have seen that the wise men represent the many peoples who will pay tribute to God, and that in one passage from the prophet Isaiah there is a mention of gold and incense being brought to give honour to the Lord. That passage does not mention the wise men's third gift, the gift of myrrh. Against the background of joy, delight and homage, the myrrh sounds an ominous note. Myrrh is a highly fragrant plant resin. It was expensive, and used as an ingredient in perfumes and in anointing oils; it was also often an ingredient in the scented oil used to anoint dead bodies in order to lessen the stench of decay. In Mark's Gospel, in the scene where a group of women make their way to the tomb in order to anoint the dead Jesus (Mk 16:1), there is no mention of myrrh, yet the reference to myrrh shortly after Jesus' birth sets up a clear connection with his Passion and death. It also hints at the death of the King who has only just been born. Taken together, the gifts of gold, frankincense and myrrh show that it is in the very act of acknowledging the kingship of the newborn child that the wise men inadvertently draw attention to his vulnerability to the rulers of this world. In Jesus, the all-powerful one submits himself to the powers, so that those who submit to him may be freed from the power of death.

The wise men came to Jesus as pilgrims. In anticipating the procession of the nations to Christ, they also anticipated the countless men and women who would travel on pilgrimage in order to grow in their faith. Even today, travel can be an inconvenience, but then it was a highly dangerous inconvenience. At the time of Christ, travel involved something more than just forsaking the routines and comforts of home. Saint Paul, referring to his missionary travels, wrote of his experience of 'danger from rivers, danger from bandits ... danger in the city, danger in the wilderness ...' (2 Cor 11:26). Travel was not something to be undertaken lightly: it was a matter of vocation rather than vacation. Pope John Paul II, in a letter to prepare for the second millennium Jubilee of Christ's birth, wrote that the whole Christian life is a 'pilgrimage to the house of the Father'. The late Pope borrowed this imagery from the parable of the Prodigal Son, in which the young man, having wandered far from his father's loving care, determined to arise and return to his father's house. In a very real sense, for believers, travel is compulsory – to be a Christian is to be on pilgrimage, it is to acknowledge that 'here we have no lasting city, but we are looking for the city that is to come' (Heb 13:14). Setting out from their home in the East, the wise men did not have the clarity that is given to those who have encountered Christ, yet they had a wise restlessness, which expressed itself in pilgrimage.

If the wise men undertook their pilgrimage at the prompting of the Spirit, they were no less open to the Spirit in the manner in which they concluded it. The Gospel of Matthew tells us that 'having been warned in a dream not to return to Herod, they left for their own country by another road'. The opening lines of Robert Frost's poem, 'The Bearer of Evil Tidings', reflect something of the situation which obliged the wise men to change their travel plans:

> The bearer of evil tidings,
> When he was halfway there,
> Remembered that evil tidings
> Were a dangerous thing to bear.

From Herod's perspective, the wise men returning from Bethlehem brought evil tidings. Sadly and perversely, where he could have found cause to 'rejoice exceedingly with great joy,' Herod instead entered a paroxysm of rage. But God's providence is ahead of human machinations, and having been warned in their dream, the wise men consented to a change of itinerary. In addition to their determination, which brought them all the way to Bethlehem, the wise men show flexibility in allowing their plans to be changed. They differ radically with Herod on two counts: their homage contrasts with Herod's homicidal anger, and their openness to God's promptings contrasts with Herod's obstinate refusal even to consider that God might be working in the events which had drawn the wise men from the East.

In the New Testament, there is another significant change of itinerary – one that bears some striking similarities to that of the wise men. In the Acts of the Apostles (16:6-10) we read how, at a particular point during his missionary travels, one of the travelling companions of Saint Paul noted that the Spirit of Jesus had interfered with Paul's missionary itinerary. Whereas Paul and his companions had planned to continue their broad sweep of present-day Turkey in keeping with a certain geographical logic, the Spirit prevented them from doing this. We are not given any details, but whatever concrete events scuttled their original plan, Saint Paul and his fellow missionaries interpreted the setback as the prompting of the Holy Spirit, and they decided to travel west instead of north. This change of itinerary had extremely far-reaching consequences: the small group of missionaries made their way to the port town of Troas, and there they made the passage from Asia Minor across to Europe. Thus began Paul's proclamation of the Gospel in a new continent. We can only speculate how Church history might read if Paul had clung obstinately to his original project, and failed to read an apparent setback as the work of the Holy Spirit.

This incident, along with the route-change of the wise men, reminds us that perseverance in heeding the promptings of the Holy Spirit is more important than perseverance in following a fixed itinerary. Life offers us steady reminders of the fact that 'for now we see in a mirror, dimly' (1 Cor 13:12), and our faith is at its best, not when it is a pursuit of certainty-at-all-costs, but when it helps us to bend with the breeze and roll with the punches.

A line from Psalm 95 reads: 'O come, let us worship and bow down, let us kneel before the Lord, our Maker!' On entering the stable of Bethlehem, the wise men accepted this invitation. They had never heard this line from the Psalm; they had no previous contact with the religious tradition of Israel – a tradition which was open to the coming of a Messiah. In a certain sense, we can say that the wise men 'appeared out of nowhere'. That a band of wealthy men from the East should drop in on a newborn child in Bethlehem bearing expensive gifts is, to put it mildly, rather improbable. Yet once they have paid their homage and offered their gifts, the same men disappear from the Gospel just as promptly as they had appeared. Aside from the detail that they returned to their country by a different road, we hear nothing further about them: any hint of Eastern promise, any anticipation that the wise men might go and tell others about the newborn King, disappears without trace.

The wisdom shown by the wise men is not unlimited. Evidently, they are men of good will, yet they represent the quintessentially modern phenomenon of believing without belonging. Indeed, the wise men bear a striking similarity to those who 'practice their faith at Christmas time', then disappear as quickly as they have appeared. They have been drawn, intrigued, fascinated, but they have not been captivated. Their mysterious and short-lived presence in the Gospel story offers us both a consolation and a challenge. Jesus Christ is for all. He is not the Lord of the virtuous, the pious, the observant, the practicing, but the Lord of all. It is consoling indeed to reflect that God's providence and love for every person simply does not admit to being tied down by all-too-human distinctions such as practicing or non-practicing, member or non-member. God is a lover, not a lawyer, and admission to the manger is free.

On a more challenging note, the wise men remind us that departure from the manger is also free, and that having encountered the Lord, we are at liberty to return to a life that is untouched by his presence. It is, in fact, the adult Christ that wins men and women: the Christ who spoke and healed and suffered and died, the Christ who overcame death. The best that the crib can do is revive our nostalgia, sharpen our longing for a real encounter with the Risen Lord. But we remain free to pursue this encounter or not to do so; the Lord invites but never imposes.

Points to ponder

+ The wise men are free, yet fascinated. At one and the same time, God both respects their liberty and draws them irresistibly. It is their very freedom that is captivated by what God is doing. Believers can fall victim to confused notions of freedom, to the point of seeing discipleship as placing a limit on freedom, but God's appeal to our freedom is simply the appeal of love. People who have fallen in love do not imagine themselves to have lost their freedom; on the contrary, to love is to learn what freedom is for. In the appearance and departure of the wise men, we see the graciousness of a God who invites but does not impose, the patience of a God who waits serenely for individuals and for all of humanity.

+ God does not suffer anxiety, but the same cannot be said for the world! Our age is an age of anxiety for human society and its future, an ecological or even cosmic anxiety for the future of our planet. The crib speaks consolingly to this anxiety. The wise men remind us that in God's vocabulary, 'humanity' and 'family' are the same word, and that God's ultimate plan is to bless all people, even those who seem furthest from him. The star which proclaims the birth of Christ also proclaims the fact that the cosmos is under God's authority, and all its movements are caught up in God's unfolding plan. We are invited to bring all our anxieties – whether for the human family or for our suffering planet – to the Son of God, born for us in the humility of Bethlehem.

+ 'I am convinced that neither death, nor life, nor angels, nor rulers, nor things present, nor things to come, nor powers,

nor height, nor depth, nor anything else in all creation, will
be able to separate us from the love of God in Christ Jesus
our Lord.' So writes Saint Paul in his letter to the Romans
(8:38-39). Not only can nothing come between us and
God's love: by God's unfathomable providence, everything
conspires in our favour. God is at the end of every journey,
every pilgrimage, every ordeal, and so we can make our own
the confident resolution of the prophet Habakkuk (3:17):
'Though the fig tree does not blossom, and no fruit is on the
vines; though the produce of the olive fails and the fields
yield no food; though the flock is cut off from the fold and
there is no herd in the stall, yet I will rejoice in the Lord.'

Chapter Four

Disturbing the Tyrant: The Anger of King Herod

> When he laughed, respectable senators burst
> with laughter,
> And when he cried the little children died
> in the streets.
>
> W. H. Auden (1907–1973)

These lines from W. H. Auden's short poem, 'Epitaph on a Tyrant', are well suited to the homicidal King Herod. They also remind us of the fact that there is nothing far-fetched or incredible about the description in Matthew's Gospel of Herod's reaction to the news of Christ's birth. Can this minor Middle-Eastern potentate really have sought to eliminate a newborn baby by an act of indiscriminate slaughter? Both history and human nature assure us that sadly the answer to this question is affirmative: if Herod was unmeasured in his determination to stamp out any threat to his power, his actions were merely in keeping with those of many a despot before and since.

Yet Herod is no scapegoat for the evil that is present in every human heart. While we may contemplate his actions with horror, we should not overlook the more genteel and cultured manifestations of evil that we can, with a decent pinch of honesty, find within ourselves. These lines from Adam Zagajewski's poem, 'Escalator', can apply to more than just the Herods of history:

> Why should the cities be vanquished,
> Why hurl stones and ravage shrines,
> When scorn, whispers, and laughter will suffice?

But why include Herod in our reflections, when he is not part of the proceedings? We do not, after all, put a statue of Herod somewhere between the ox and one of the shepherds – he simply does not belong there. This may be true, but the fact of the matter is that Herod figures prominently in the proceedings, as recounted in Matthew's Gospel. Whether we like it or not, Herod's passion and cunning are part of the story. While we may not represent Herod visually in our cribs, he is nonetheless a key player. Some reflection on the figure of Herod can also keep us mindful of the nature of Christ's love: it was because of his great love that the Lord, from the beginning of his life on earth to its ending on the cross, willingly endured threats and opposition.

Who was this Herod, so threatened by news of the birth of an infant? To historians, he is known as Herod the Great, father of the Herod who plays a role in the events surrounding Christ's Passion. Herod the Great was the ruler of Jewish Palestine from 37 BC until just a couple of years after Christ's birth. Politically, Herod was hugely successful. A ruthless, conniving figure, the formula behind his political success was loyalty to self in the guise of loyalty to Rome. According to a prominent historian of the time, Herod was lavish beyond measure in courting Roman approval and support: he was a master of the tactic of self-serving generosity. Herod had cleverly invoked Roman support in the course of domestic political difficulties, and he was rewarded by being crowned king of Judaea during a visit to Rome. Subsequently, he survived a war with a neighbouring country, a devastating earthquake in Judaea, and the political demise of Anthony, his patron in Rome.

Herod was brought up on political intrigue, his father having been killed by political opponents. In his turn, Herod had gone on to eliminate those who stood between him and his goals – even to the point of resolving marital difficulties by having his wife executed. He was politically astute and unerringly loyal to his political masters, in many ways the model regional ruler, as far as Rome was concerned.

Little wonder, then, that King Herod was troubled by the news that some foreign dignitaries were present in Jerusalem and seeking to pay homage to a newborn king, whom they described as the King of the Jews. Was not Herod king in these parts? He was in charge of all the country's institutions, including the Sanhedrin (at that time, the nearest thing to a Jewish parliament in Jerusalem), and the high priesthood. If anyone could match the description 'King of the Jews', as far as Herod was concerned, it was him and no other. From Herod's perspective, the wise men's question, 'Where is the child who has been born king of the Jews?' conveyed a threat, a menace, a real and present danger. Any pretender to Herod's throne would have to be eliminated, and it is this murderous intent that informs Herod's dealings with the wise men.

There is a huge contrast between the attitude of the visitors coming from the East to pay homage, and the paranoia of Herod. The former are nearing the end of their journey; the latter is beginning to plot the elimination of a child. The former are on the verge of great delight; the latter is slipping into a murderous rage. Herod is the most serious man in the story: he is full of his own importance. In this fullness, there is no room for anyone else. Herod shows us evil in its purest form: self-absorption. It is the gravity of his self-importance that motivates him to destroy. He reminds us that, as G. K. Chesterton puts it, 'Satan fell by the force of gravity'. In the same context, Chesterton observed that 'angels can fly because they take themselves lightly'. Perhaps those words convey something of the lightness of spirit that enabled the wise men to undertake their long journey. No such attitude is found in Herod, who is a dark and terrible burden to himself and others.

It is worth spelling out the fact that Herod was frightened by the news of Jesus' birth, not because he was a weak man who feared judgment, but because he was a powerful man who feared opposition. Herod's problem was not so much immorality, as autonomy. The child lying in the manger a short distance from Jerusalem was not a dread judge, waiting to stamp out every human weakness. Rather, he was the embodiment of a new kind of kingship: a kingship of humility and service. But Herod was not interested in enquiring what kind of king had been born. For him, it was enough that there was a pretender to his throne, one who would have to be eliminated.

Interestingly, Herod reacts to the perceived threat to his autonomy by calling a meeting of the chief priests and scribes, so that he can enlist their help in locating the newborn opponent to the throne. There is a rather odd contrast between Herod's demonic sense of autonomy and his acknowledgement of his need for help in maintaining it. If the safeguarding of his position entails a momentary dependence upon others, so be it – Herod will not shrink from this. The meeting between Herod and the religious leaders anticipates the plotting between the chief priests and leaders of the people that will take place shortly before Jesus' death (Mt 26:3-4). Here, we see the dark shadow of the cross falling across the joyous event of the birth of Christ.

It is also striking that the only item of information Herod seeks is the child's whereabouts. He could have taken advantage of the gathering to ask the assembled religious leaders about the expectation of a kingly figure; he could have sought to understand. But neither context nor circumstance are relevant to the one whose mind is fixed and closed; all he needs is to locate his target. There is not the faintest suggestion of a pause for thought or for self-examination – less still is there any hint of self-doubt. Herod is single-minded and a man of action. While these may, at times, be admirable qualities, they can be utterly destructive in those who bow to no one other than themselves.

Of the four Gospels, is it Mark's that is generally considered the one that stresses opposition to Jesus at the earliest point in his story and in the most ominous manner. As early as the beginning of chapter two of Mark's Gospel, some religious leaders express the view that Jesus is a blasphemer, a charlatan rather than a man of genuine piety. But Matthew's Christmas story sounds a note of opposition just as early on, and just as starkly. In Matthew's Gospel, like Mark's, the opposition appears in the second chapter. But Matthew allows the shadow of the cross to fall across the manger, rather than over the beginning of the Lord's public ministry. At the beginning of Jesus' life, the violent opposition of Herod and his collusion with the religious leaders anticipate the circumstances that will lead to Jesus' execution.

Having consulted with the religious leaders, Herod invites the wise men to a meeting. It is, we are told, a secret meeting. Evil requires the cover of darkness and secrecy. The oxygen of iniquity is distortion, guardedness, the half-truth. But all of these things can be presented with great panache, and one can imagine the serpentine charm with which Herod welcomed his unsuspecting guests. Herod was, of course, long practiced in the use of the charm offensive: over the years, he had used it to gain and to preserve the support of his Roman masters. Now, he uses all his persuasive powers to insinuate himself into the wise men's plan: 'Go and search diligently for the child,' he tells them, 'and when you have found him, bring me word so that I may also go and pay him homage' (Mt 2:8).

In order to appreciate the subtlety of evil and the wonders of God's unfolding plan, we can reflect on how evil attempts to gain a foothold, even as God's plan is reaching its high point. The wise men have all but completed their journey. They have been guided by gentle promptings and vague intuitions; they are now on the verge of finding the one whom they seek. Just as this part of the story seems poised to reach a happy conclusion, an evil character enters the plot. He threatens to undo God's plan and render purposeless the goodwill, longing and searching of the wise men. This is high drama, and it introduces into the Christmas story what turns out to be a universal rule of God's providence: 'Where sin increased, grace abounded all the more' (Rom 5:20). Sin will increase. In fact, it has a tendency to do so at crucial moments in the working out of God's saving plan. But God will not be outdone, and his grace is always a step ahead. Indeed, grace races far ahead of sin.

Herod's plan of destruction is now, he thinks and hopes, fixed like a parasite to the benevolent intentions of the wise men. But as soon as the wise men leave Herod's presence, they set out and see the star ahead of them. They had not seen this heavenly body since its rising in the East, but now, just as the power of evil rears its head, the star reappears. The Gospel gives us no reason to assume that the wise men were accompanied by any external signs during their journey to Jerusalem: they travelled by the light of desire, rather than by the light of the star. It is just when the force of evil is alerted to what God is doing, that God himself intervenes to tackle a power that is too strong and conniving for people of goodwill to overcome without assistance. We see the same pattern at work after the wise men have visited the newborn Jesus. They do not spot Herod's duplicity for themselves, but are warned in a dream not to return to him. It is God himself who deals with the power of evil. The human task is trustful obedience.

On discovering that he has been duped, Herod flies into a rage and orders a mass execution of children, in the hope that the newborn king will not slip through his net. By this time, Joseph has been warned in a dream, and has fled to Egypt with the child and his mother. But Herod does not know this, and so the impotent vanity of his murderous resistance to God's plan is made plain. In the Old Testament, just as God was calling the Jews to be a people for himself, his Chosen People, the Egyptian Pharaoh set about killing all the first-born males of the Jews (Ex 1). The murderous anger of Herod at the birth of Christ shows us that the response of evil to God's plans is predictable and unchanging. Also unchanging, however, is God's ability to deal with opposition. The whole Herod affair is marked, as we noted, by high drama, but the outcome is never in doubt.

Points to ponder

✦ There is a striking contrast between the sheer malevolence of King Herod's machinations and the gratuitous goodness of God's plans. From moment to moment, as the story unfolds, it can appear as though Herod is gaining the upper hand. Of course, we know the story and we know that Christ is preserved from harm ... at least for now. Yet we might with some justice describe it as a close call. Herod was utterly determined: he seems to have been successful in convincing the wise men of his *bona fides*, and he is willing to do whatever it takes to preserve his position from threat. There are times when evil seems able to keep pace with good, to the point of looking poised to overtake it altogether. There are times when evil seems to be given free reign, as we see in the episode of the slaughter of the innocents. Nobody can presume to offer ready answers to the apparent triumphs of evil, but the story of Herod and his scheming tells us several things about evil: it is very real and very powerful; it can be present at the very heart of the outworking of God's plans; it will have moments of real triumph; it will ultimately fail.

✦ What kingdoms of ours are threatened by real openness to God's plan? What little totalitarianism of ego or addiction might we fear having invaded by the power of grace? Herod can represent that part of committed believers, which fears that God wants to overthrow, to capture, and to destroy our independence. A large part of the journey of Christian maturity is growth in the realisation that God wants our freedom. It is only in God that the kingdom of human happiness and peace can be established, and God wants to establish rather than overthrow. He allows us to resist his plans, because he wants to captivate rather than capture. But even as we resist – perhaps successfully for a time – God has other ways of appealing to us, of reaching us, of breaking through our defences.

+ Herod was, it seems, more than a match for the wise men; he was well able to outsmart them with his practiced charm. The only person in the Gospel fully able to deal with Herod's deception is God himself, acting through the intermediary of dreams. There is a tendency in disciples to seek to root out evil, whether it is found in ourselves or in others. But only God can deal with evil in a definitive way. In cooperation with God's grace, we may experience lesser or greater victories in our struggle with evil and sin, but the power and the allure of evil remain, and the final victory depends entirely on God. Jesus makes this very clear in his parable about weeds, which have been planted by an enemy and are now growing vigorously in a field of wheat (Mt 13:24-30). When an enthusiastic servant offers to pull out the weeds, his master tells him to leave them until harvest time. The weeds will be dealt with in due course, but in accordance with the master's timetable. God's dealings with Herod can invite each of us to trust that God will, in his way and at his time, deal fully and definitively with everything that troubles and distresses his children.

Chapter Five

Good News of Great Joy: The Message of the Angels

> Angels we have heard on high
> Sweetly singing o'er the plains
> And the mountains in reply
> Echoing their joyous strains
> Gloria in excelsis Deo
>> Translated by James Chadwick from the French
>> original by H. F. Hémy (1818–1888)

Did the angelic host actually sing, or do these well-known lines offer another example of pious embellishment? The Gospel does not tell us that the angels broke into song, but it leaves us in no doubt that they broke out in prose! 'Glory to God in the highest heaven, and on earth, peace among those whom he favours' (Lk 2:14). This is not simply a statement of fact: it is a soaring hymn of wonder and praise. It is, to say the very least, poetry rather than prose. That the Gospel breaks into poetic language is very telling. There are certain events that just cannot be adequately conveyed in ordinary language, and the birth of Christ is one such event – indeed, it is the event *par excellence*.

It is in the Gospel of Luke that we read about the appearance of the angels to the shepherds. Interestingly, Luke opens his Gospel with one of the longest and most elegantly structured sentences in the entire New Testament. This Gospel is addressed to an eminent individual named Theophilus, and Luke is concerned from the beginning that he win the confidence of his distinguished reader by showing a flair for polished language. Yet, Luke knows that when it comes to communicating the wonderful events surrounding the birth of Christ, even the most elegant Greek prose is inadequate. By the end of the first chapter of his Gospel, his story twice breaks into song. The first departure from straightforward prose is the song of Mary, her Magnificat, a rapturous hymn in praise of God's deeds. Just a few verses later, Zechariah reacts to the birth of his son, John the Baptist, by uttering the poetic prophecy known as the Benedictus. In the second chapter of Luke's Gospel there is a further eruption from prose to poetry, with the proclamation of the angels.

The Good News has a vitality and an energy that cannot be expressed in plain language, and this is just as it should be. If the birth of Christ marks the beginning of our salvation, then it is – or should be – music to the ears of humanity. The events of the first Christmas cannot be adequately communicated in the terse language of the press statement: they must be proclaimed in song. Little wonder, then, that the singing of carols is a beloved element of the celebration of Christmas.

The angel who speaks to the shepherds is not the first angel to appear in Luke's Gospel. An unnamed angel has already appeared to Zechariah, and the angel Gabriel has visited Mary in Nazareth. Near the very end of the Gospel, two figures in dazzling clothes appear at Christ's empty tomb on Easter morning. They are understood to be divine messengers, sent to proclaim Christ's resurrection from the dead. What all these figures have in common is their task of communication: they are sent to let people know that God himself is at work, intervening in human affairs, bringing wonderful things to pass. Many cribs have an angel above them, bearing a sign that reads, *Gloria in excelsis Deo*. In truth, this sign could equally well read, 'God at work'.

In our opening chapter, we saw how the crib captures some of the earliest Christian counter-propaganda. The angel told the shepherds that they would find in Bethlehem a child who was Saviour and Lord. At the time the Gospel was written, these titles were being applied more and more exclusively to the Roman Emperor; they were already, we might say, the property of Caesar Augustus. But now they are being appropriated – Caesar might say, 'stolen' – by an infant.

When they appear to the shepherds, the angels bring a message of peace, but that very message also throws down the gauntlet to Rome. The angels proclaim that the imperial order is to be stood on its head; the only plan that really matters will unfold not in power and prestige, but in weakness and humility. Lordship will no longer be synonymous with opulence, nor salvation with a programme of political ruthlessness. Instead, Lordship is found in poverty, and salvation begins with disarming gentleness.

Even at his birth, this child has begun to 'cast the mighty from their thrones and lift up the lowly', to borrow the language of Mary's Magnificat. Mary sensed that God's plan was to involve a reordering of the powers of this world. Her intuition is confirmed by the angel's insistence that her child Jesus is Lord and Saviour. While the Gospel does not present Jesus as a direct threat to Roman imperial power, this is precisely how he and his followers will be understood in due course. The subsequent clash of world-views will lead to centuries of intermittent persecution, until Christianity finally becomes the official religion of the empire, early in the fourth century.

'Peace on earth' is at the heart of the angel's greeting to the shepherds. Yet the child whose birth is being proclaimed will grow up to say, 'Do you think that I have come to bring peace to the earth? No, I tell you, but rather division!' (Lk 12:51) What kind of peace is being announced? How can the newborn Jesus be a sign and a promise of peace, if his arrival will arouse the wrath of Rome and if he himself will promise division? The answer is found in Jesus' farewell speech to his disciples, in John's Gospel: 'Peace I leave with you; my peace I give to you.

I do not give to you as the world gives' (Jn 14:27). The peace announced by the angels at Christ's birth, and promised by Christ himself near the end of his life, is a peace rooted in justice rather than in political power, in right rather than in might. It is, accordingly, a peace offered to those who pursue justice, even if that pursuit sets them on a collision course with the powers of this world. It is a peace that can be established only through struggle and division. The angel's message and the later words of the adult Jesus do not invite believers to violent struggle or wilful divisiveness, but the message is clear: the peace to be established by Jesus will meet with resistance. The powers of this world have their ways and their structures – they will not consent to change without a struggle.

It is not only on the level of politics and social reality that the peace announced by the angel will prove demanding and divisive. The division promised by Christ is felt within the heart of each believer, as he or she struggles to live the words, 'Thy kingdom come, Thy will be done on earth' (Mt 6:10). However, this inner struggle will at times sound a 'call to arms' in a more external way, and the notion that Christians should be docile, passive and uncritically accepting of this world's ills can be a betrayal of the peace announced at the birth of Christ. We might think of Martin Luther King Jr, writing from a prison cell in Birmingham, Alabama, to religious leaders who had criticised him for engaging in civil rights protests that had caused social unrest. To the idea that his actions were to be condemned because they precipitated violence, King Jr replied that this would be equivalent to condemning Jesus because his unique dedication to God's will and kingdom eventually led to the evil of the crucifixion. The Prince of Peace is born indeed, but his followers are recruited as well as redeemed. The peace Christ came to bring is not the peace of indifference, nor is it a peace-at-all-costs. It is a peace arising from and rooted in justice and goodwill.

If, in a certain sense, the peace of Christ has a paradoxical military quality, this paradox is reflected in the fact that Luke's Gospel speaks of an 'army' of angels. In Luke's Greek, the 'heavenly host' is in fact an army, but one which proclaims peace on earth. Membership of this army is not confined to angels: to be a Christian is to belong to an army of faithful who engage in non-violent war with everything that is contrary to God's Kingdom of justice. In this war, it is love, not violence, that conquers.

Luke's Gospel makes it clear that the angel visits the shepherds at night-time, as they keep watch over their flocks. The angel who makes the announcement of Jesus' birth is accompanied by a great and glorious light, which terrifies the shepherds. Now, brightness at night is common, whether in the middle of a city or elsewhere. At the time of Jesus' birth, any sudden light at night would have been alarming, but the light that accompanied the angels is more than just light; it is 'the glory of the Lord', a manifestation of God's own presence. The infant Jesus will grow up to proclaim, 'I am the light of the world' (Jn 8:12), but right now, even the announcement of his birth brings 'light to those who sit in darkness' (Lk 1:79). Yes, the very mention of Jesus' birth puts darkness to flight, bringing light and hope. On the first Christmas night, the glory of the Lord shone before the shepherds had any idea of what was happening. The light of Christ is a gift for believers. It is not something that we need to generate by our own efforts: we are enlightened by God's presence and his promise, both of which come to completion in Jesus.

For a moment, let us glance ahead in Luke's Gospel, from the proclamation made by the host of angels at Jesus' birth, to the proclamation made by the crowds just a few days before his death. As Jesus entered Jerusalem, riding on a donkey, people lined the streets and acclaimed: 'Blessed is the king who comes in the name of the Lord! Peace in heaven and glory in the highest heaven' (Lk 19:38). There is an interesting discrepancy between the words of the angels at the birth of Jesus and those of the crowds on that later occasion. Whereas the angelic host proclaims glory in heaven and peace on earth, in the understanding of the crowd, both the peace and the glory are located in heaven. Why is this? It may well be that the crowd greeting Jesus failed to realise that the peace he brings is not an otherworldly matter: it is peace on earth; it is peace here and now – peace today. Jesus has not come merely to promise peace: he is peace and he brings peace with him. Those who receive him can experience something of that peace. Even in the midst of a world that clings to the way of violence, we can be confident that the Lord will 'guide our feet into the way of peace' (Lk 1:79).

The baby lying a short distance from where the shepherds are at work is, the angel declares, Saviour, Messiah and Lord. There is an enormous contrast between these impressive titles and the words of the angel which immediately follow them: 'You will find a child wrapped in bands of cloth and lying in a manger.' If God is doing great things, he is most certainly not shunning humble means. Throughout history, the avoidance of what is impressive or grandiose seems to be virtually a point of honour with God; when he brings great things to pass, he does so without recourse to great things. What is more, it is the very contrast between the exalted titles of Jesus and his lowly state as an infant in a manger that causes the heavenly host to break into praise: only God's transcendent wisdom could draw together meekness and might, humility and majesty, in the manner of the first Christmas night. To God be all the glory!

In greeting the shepherds, the angel uses an ordinary word which in Luke's Gospel has an extraordinary importance. The one who is Saviour, Messiah and Lord is born, the angel tells us, today. The word 'today' is the first word spoken by Jesus in the synagogue at Nazareth after he reads from the scriptures – in effect, it is the first word of his public ministry. Having read from the scroll of the prophet Isaiah, Jesus announces to the congregation: 'Today this scripture has been fulfilled in your hearing' (Lk 4:21). Upon reading a text which promises wonderful blessings from God – blessings for the poor, the captive, the blind and the oppressed – Jesus proceeds to assure his hearers that these words are now, today, coming to fruition. What is more, it is in Jesus himself that the blessing is being offered. Importantly, the word 'today' also concludes the public ministry of Jesus. As he hangs upon the cross, Jesus tells the thief hanging next to him: 'Truly I tell you, today you will be with me in paradise' (Lk 23:43).

It is not by accident that Luke's Gospel locates the earthly ministry of Jesus between these two uses of the word 'today'. Jesus touches lives concretely, here and now, not in some vague manner and at a time unknown. When Jesus met Zacchaeus, that diminutive tax collector who had climbed up a tree so that he could see over the heads of the crowd, Jesus said to him, 'Zacchaeus, hurry and come down, for I must stay at your house today' (Lk 19:5). In response to the self-righteous grumblers who resented Jesus' kindness towards Zacchaeus, Jesus insisted, 'Today, salvation has come to this house' (Lk 19:9). In these words spoken to Zacchaeus, Jesus lets us know that when we encounter him, our lives are changed now. As believers, we have more than just a promise of paradise, an eternal destiny, a tomorrow: because of Jesus, we have a fresh today. At the first Christmas, Jesus came to stay with humanity, and the angel's announcement reminds us that in Jesus, God blesses us today; not two millennia ago, nor in some vague future, but here and now.

Points to ponder

+ There is great wisdom for us in the fact that the birth of Christ causes the Gospel to break out of prose and into poetry and song. Words are terribly important, but they can carry us only so far. In fact, words never arrive at the final station: no relationship, no friendship, no love can be entirely captured by words. Poetry and song can certainly reach further than prose, but even they have their limits. Many committed believers are keenly aware that when it comes to their attempts to pray, words do not carry them sufficiently far. From this, people sometimes conclude that they are unable to pray. It is far more likely, however, that a sense of inability to pray is a sign that prayer is encountering the limitation of words, and seeking to move beyond them. At the first Christmas, the angels sang of Christ's birth. More routinely, believers groan at their inability to reach Christ in prayer. But the groans of believers are themselves a very deep prayer. Saint Paul reassures us of this: 'We ourselves, who have the first fruits of the Holy Spirit, groan inwardly ...' (Rom 8:23). In fact Saint Paul's reassurance goes even deeper: he tells us that we really do not know how to pray as we ought, but that the Spirit 'intercedes for us with sighs too deep for words' (Rom 8:26). Just as at the first Christmas, so too in our own day the Lord is doing more for his people than words can describe. In response, we can make our own the acclamation of the angels, or we can groan, or simply be silent, gratefully accepting that the Spirit intercedes within us.

✦ The brilliance which shone around the angel on the first Christmas night was the brilliance of Christ himself, of the one who was to say, 'I am the light of the world'. But Christ also says to us, his followers, 'You are the light of the world ... let your light shine before others' (Mt 5:14, 16). Light has become central to the celebration of Christmas – even in the most secular celebrations. Every Christmas illumination, whether prominently positioned in a shop window, or almost hidden within a crib, can remind us of how blessed we are to know Christ Jesus, to walk by the light of his promise, a promise that enlightens us here and now, today. This promise also holds out a challenge to us: to be a light for our sisters and brothers, to be peacemakers, to bring encouragement, to bear with limitations, to reflect something of Christ's own light.

✢ What is the point of faith, of Church? At times, almost the whole significance of religion risks being reduced to 'getting people into heaven', while the equally important task of 'getting heaven into people' is virtually overlooked. But Christ is born today; he visits us today, he wants to stay with us today, to make a difference now, in this life and not just in the next. It is because the reality of Christ is ever-present, always today, that we can encounter him in the present. After his resurrection, Jesus spoke to two of his disciples about the meaning of his suffering and death. When he took his leave of them, they were able to say, 'Were not our hearts burning within us, while he was talking to us?' (Lk 24:32). We, too, can encounter Christ in each of our 'todays' – we can hear his voice and experience his word as something real and effective. We can hope that when the eternal 'today' dawns for us, we might be worthy of a lovely epitaph once composed for an ordinary, unremarkable believer: 'Of this good man let this praise be given: heaven was in him before he was in heaven.'

Chapter Six

'Let us go and see': The Visit of the Shepherds

> The shepherds at those tidings
> Rejoiced much in mind
> And left their flocks a-feeding
> In tempest storms of wind
> And straight they came to Bethlehem
> The Son of God to find
> And it's tidings of comfort and joy.
>
> Anonymous

It is often thought that shepherds at the time of Christ were regarded with suspicion, that they were considered rough, uncouth men, strangers to respectable society. A very different view, found in some literature dating from even before the time of Christ, tends to idealise the figure of the shepherd, seeing him as the model of a primitive, peaceful, uncorrupted life. We need not speculate on which of these views is more accurate, for this much is clear: shepherds were poor, and they were marginal. The nature of their job kept them away from town and village life, and while some shepherds may have owned small holdings on which they kept their flocks, there is no doubt that they were at the lower end of the socio-economic spectrum.

Between them, the Gospels of Matthew and Luke bring two sets of visitors to the manger, but the contrast between Matthew's well-heeled Magi and Luke's down-at-heel shepherds could scarcely be greater. Taken together, these two sets of visitors let us know that there is room in the manger for everyone, the rich and the poor and all those in between. But whereas one might have expected to find the cultured and the well-to-do paying their respects to a newborn king, the presence of those from the lowest reaches of society is surprising. The contrast is due in part to the differing needs of the audiences for whom Matthew and Luke wrote their Gospels, and it is worth considering these differences for a moment, in order to underline the fact that the good news of the birth of Christ is for everyone, regardless of where they may be located along the spectrum of human approval or respectability.

Matthew, it seems, wrote his Gospel for a community in which there were plenty of people who had no shortage of life's necessities. In composing his Gospel, he took care to ensure that the better-off people in his audience would not feel excluded. This concern is seen especially in the way that Matthew makes slight alterations to some of the Beatitudes: whereas in Luke's Gospel we read, 'Blessed are you who are poor' (Lk 6:20), the equivalent phrase in Matthew reads, 'Blessed are the poor in spirit' (Mt 5:3). Again, where Luke's Gospel reads, 'Blessed are you who are hungry' (Lk 6:21), Matthew's Gospel reads, 'Blessed are those who hunger and thirst for righteousness' (Mt 5:6). In making these adjustments to sayings which both he and Luke reported, Matthew is driving home the point that the good news of Jesus is also for those who are well-off. Another indicator of the different concerns of Matthew and Luke is the very obvious fact that Matthew deems his purpose to be well served by his interest in the wealthy visitors to the manger, whereas Luke focuses attention on poorer visitors.

Luke's Gospel shows a special interest in the poor and the outcast. Jesus begins his public ministry by telling people that he has come 'to bring good news to the poor' (Lk 4:18). Some of the parables in this Gospel make it clear that wealth can bring its own risks: the parable of the rich fool (Lk 12:16-21) warns against finding security in riches; the parable of the rich man and Lazarus (Lk 16:19-31) insists that riches will lead to doom unless they are generously shared. But even in Luke's Gospel, Jesus reaches out to those who are wealthy, as we can see in his attitude to the wealthy tax collector, Zacchaeus, to whom he offers the gift of salvation. While there is nothing exclusive or rigid in its approach, Luke's Gospel plainly has a soft spot for the poor, the marginal and the vulnerable. By bringing the shepherds to the manger, Luke tells us that our poverty and our vulnerability are welcome there. We do not have to be wealthy or wise; we do not have to be polished or cultured; we do not have to come bearing gifts. What we are asked to bring to the crib is our self, 'warts and all'. The special welcome that the child in the crib extends to human weakness is beautifully captured in some lines from Christina Rossetti's poem, 'A Christmas Carol':

> What can I give Him,
> Poor as I am?
> If I were a shepherd
> I would bring a lamb,
> If I were a wise man
> I would do my part, –
> Yet what can I give him,
> Give my heart.

If there is a great contrast between Luke's shepherds and Matthew's Magi, there is an even greater one between the shepherds and the person of Caesar Augustus, who is mentioned in Luke's Gospel just a few verses before the shepherds. We have already seen something of the irony in the fact that Caesar, the most powerful man in the world, is quite peripheral to the story of Christ's birth. For all his works and all his pomp, Caesar does not amount to anything more than historical background. The real action is taking place elsewhere, in humble places and in humble people. The irony of Caesar's insignificance is greatly underlined by the fact that some shepherds are the first to hear of Christ's birth. The birth of the King is announced, not to the emperor, but to some men whom society deems to be of no consequence. The fact that the angel's announcement is made to mere shepherds inverts every form of snobbery; it makes fun of every notion of self-importance; it derides the pretensions of every 'in-group'. The shepherds near Bethlehem were lowly men going about their ordinary work when heaven broke in to their ordinariness. The good news came to them as pure gift and complete surprise. And it came to them by God's free, sovereign choice.

The consequences for the life of discipleship are clear: everything is grace, nothing is earned. Christian faith and living are not a reaching out to God through some kind of moral or spiritual athleticism; rather, the life of faith is an acceptance of God's blessing. It is God who does the reaching out, just as the angel's message reached the unimportant and unsuspecting shepherds.

Lowliness is drawn to lowliness, just as surely as it is repelled by haughtiness and grandeur. It is precisely because the circumstances of Christ's birth were so humble that the shepherds could be drawn into the event. Anybody could gain access to a cattle shed, whereas only the elite could present themselves to the governing powers. Still today, the further one moves along the social spectrum, the more inaccessible people become, and those who are at the pinnacle of power and influence are almost entirely beyond the reach of ordinary citizens. The involvement of the shepherds in the story of Christ's birth conveys the sheer accessibility of God. In Christ, a new kind of king has come: one who is utterly available. The shepherds found this king surrounded by ordinariness, not by red tape or by elaborate security. They remind us that the believer's access to Christ is free and spontaneous, calling for an attitude of simple trust.

The shepherds could be regarded as outsiders in a double sense. Not only are they marginal to society, but they are completely unconnected with the family of the newborn child. One does not generally expect visits from total strangers at the time of a child's birth: unwritten and unspoken convention makes it clear that visiting is restricted to family and friends, to people with a connection. The presence of individuals who would normally be regarded as complete outsiders lets us know that the birth of Jesus is a blessing not just for a single family or group of families – it is a blessing for all. At the crib, there are no outsiders.

'Do not be afraid!' The angel Gabriel spoke these words to Mary when he visited her in Nazareth. Now, on the night of Christ's birth, the shepherds hear the same command. Why should the proclamation of good news need to begin with a command not to fear? If Gabriel and his colleague are bearing glad tidings, why should those whom they visit feel unease or even, in the case of the shepherds, terror? The most immediate and obvious reason for the shepherds' fear is the unexpected vision of the angel, along with the brilliance that shone around this heavenly figure. This was something the shepherds had not seen before; it was – to say the least – very surprising. An element of shock is to be expected when one is confronted with the utterly unexpected.

There is, however, a deeper reason for the shepherds' reaction of fear. They were being confronted not simply with the unexpected, but with the supernatural, with a manifestation of God's very own majesty. A creaturely fear is an entirely natural response to the supernatural. We are creatures of flesh and blood; of matter and time. God, while closer to us than we are to ourselves, is at the same time infinitely beyond us. A direct encounter with the divine is akin to a pulse of energy that overloads and overwhelms; it is like a weight of glory that is too much for body, mind and spirit to cope with. We are, our faith tells us, made for God; yet for our frail human nature, God is too much to bear. The presence of God instils both fear and fascination, and so the command not to fear is a merciful word of encouragement to the awestruck shepherds.

The natural, creaturely fear and trembling in the presence of God is compounded by the fact that when God reveals himself, he does not do so merely in order to impress his creatures with his transcendent majesty; when God breaks into time and space, he does so in order to *communicate*. To put it plainly: when God turns up, he turns up with a plan. And God's plan is just that – God's plan and not our plan; we cannot verify it or test it against our experience; we can only assent to it, taking a leap of faith and trust. When we apply the natural human wisdom of looking before we leap, we find ourselves peering into an abyss of mystery, and the view causes us to tremble. This is why Mary expressed hesitation and the shepherds experienced something closer to terror. This is why the angels speak the words, 'Do not be afraid'.

The shepherds' fear contrasts greatly with the angel's insistence on joy – joy at the news that the one who is Saviour, Messiah and Lord has been born. This news is no mere item of information; it invites participation, and so the shepherds are urged to go and see for themselves. No, they will not perceive the full reality of what God is doing; mystery will remain. But they will, the angel assures them, see a sign: 'a child, wrapped in bands of cloth and lying in a manger.' Earlier, the angel Gabriel had given Mary the news that her cousin, Elizabeth, was six months pregnant. Mary lost no time in making her way to see this encouraging sign of God's action: the Gospel tells us that she went 'with haste' to visit her cousin (Lk 1:39).

Now it is the shepherds' turn to hurry off and find the newborn child (the Gospel uses the same expression, 'with haste', for Mary and the shepherds). The good news does not invite a 'wait and see' approach. The validity of God's plan is not confirmed by any source outside of itself; it is experienced by those who accept God's word generously and trustingly. Of course discretion and discernment are important, but occasionally it is the angels that urge us to rush where our folly would have us fear to tread. Not so, the shepherds: as soon as the angels leave them, they hold a remarkably brief conference, which concludes with the resolution: 'Let us go now to Bethlehem and see this thing which the Lord has made known to us' (Lk 2:15).

When they arrive at the manger, the shepherds do not perceive a Saviour, Messiah and Lord. They do not see the full reality of what God is about, but only an infant – just as the angel had told them. Yet this tiny, humble sign is enough! God's plan is so vast, his promise so great, that the mere suggestion of what he is about, the slightest sign, suffices to fill the visiting shepherds with rejoicing and delight. At the sight of the infant, these humble men become like the angels who had appeared to them a short time before. The angels, Luke's Gospel tells us, had praised God and proclaimed his glory. Now the shepherds return, 'glorifying and praising God for all they had seen and heard' (Lk 2:20). Having gone to see the sign, the shepherds have themselves become a sign: these rustic men go back to work with an angelic spring in their step, having told everyone what they themselves have been told about the child in the manger. The enthusiasm of the shepherds anticipates the attitude of the group of seventy disciples, as they return to Jesus from their first mission. The Gospel tells us that these early missionaries 'returned with joy' (Lk 10:17), having experienced for themselves the validity and power of the promises made by Jesus.

There is an irresistible parallel between the shepherds leaving their flocks untended on the first Christmas night in order to find the newborn Saviour, and a shepherd who would figure in one of the Saviour's parables (Lk 15:3-7). In the parable, Jesus asks his hearers, 'Which one of you, having a hundred sheep and losing one of them, does not leave the ninety-nine in the wilderness and go after the one that is lost until he finds it?' It is a beautiful irony that on the night of the Saviour's birth, a group of shepherds abandon their flock in order to seek out the one who would later describe himself as the good shepherd, the one who 'lays down his life for the sheep' (Jn 10:11). Those who seek and find the Saviour have been sought and found by him.

Points to ponder

+ In the Gospels, the phrase 'do not fear' is the Lord's gentle, courteous acknowledgement of the fact that we are much given to fear. On being visited by angels, Mary, in spite of her generosity and openness to God, was startled; the shepherds, rough men and accustomed to danger, were struck with terror. It is a profound biblical paradox that the absence of fear is rooted in the fear of God. So much of our fear flows from our lack of sight and lack of knowledge: we most fear what we least know. But the word of God insists that 'the fear of the Lord is the beginning of knowledge' (Prov 1:7). What is this fear of God that dispels fear? In essence, 'fear of God' is a kind of biblical shorthand for the attitude that allows God to be God; the attitude that acknowledges that God is greater than our greatest crises, that he is wiser than our best insights, this his compassion exceeds our greatest kindness and sensitivity. This fear of God is not a direct answer to the questions that we may formulate in times of suffering, but it opens a perspective that allows us not to be swallowed up, crushed, by the concerns of the moment. Concerns will remain, and every heart that loves must still be a heart that bleeds, but the fear of God is an anchor and a rock of support.

+ The antithesis and indeed the antidote to fear is not so much courage, as hope. Without hope, courage can be little more than stoicism, the stiff upper lip, an attitude of grinning and bearing. Hope completes courage, by letting us know that the things that can cause fear are neither pointless nor the whole point. Negatively, the believer who has learned to hope in God knows that no suffering is beyond God's providence;

positively, she or he knows that God does not struggle to keep abreast of events, but is actively at work in all times and circumstances. The experience of the shepherds can remind us of an important source of hope. When they arrived at the place where Jesus lay, the shepherds found things to be just as the angel had told them. We have been careful to emphasise that they did not see and understand everything about the child in the manger, yet they found a congruence between what the angelic messenger had promised, and what they now experienced. There was no conflict or contradiction between the message and the reality, and this enabled the shepherds to hope that the sign they had seen at Bethlehem was just that: a sign of blessings to come. A powerful way of fostering and strengthening hope is to count one's blessings. While this phrase can be taken to refer to a form of denial, or a kind of whistling in the dark, there is no better means of growing in hope for the future than spotting and listing the signs of God's action in the past and in the present.

+ The angel raised the shepherds' sight beyond the supervision of their flocks and instilled in them a new desire. Christian faith does the same for every believer: it lifts our vision and refines our desire. It is unfortunate that many people misunderstand faith to the extent of imagining that it entails the limitation of our human desires, whereas a core Christian conviction is that we do not desire enough, but tend to limit ourselves to things that cannot satisfy. The 'Song of Songs' is the great love poem of the Bible, originally written to celebrate the love and the desire between a man and woman, but often applied to the eternal romance between God and his people. It speaks eloquently of desire, occasionally in language that relates to the experience of the shepherds. Near the beginning of the 'Song of Songs', the lover says to her beloved: 'Tell me, you whom my soul loves, where you pasture your flock, where you make it lie down at noon, for why should I be like one who is veiled beside the flocks of your companions?' (Song 1:7). The shepherds were transformed by the infusion of desire; these simple men who had been virtually enslaved to their menial task tasted something new, something higher, something finer. What the good news did for them it can do for us: impart vision, and instil desire.

Chapter Seven

Man of Righteousness and Compassion: Joseph, Son of David

Expecting? Already?
This cannot be!
Lord, can she have reneged on me?

I feared I must cast her aside
Although my love for her abides.
But now a vision bright and clear
Has bid me cast aside my fear.

Anonymous

The figure who plays Joseph in our Christmas crib is not always very well cast. He can appear just a bit too advanced in years for his particular part in the great drama which is God's saving plan. He can seem a little too delicate in his gentleness, too retiring in his silence. But the Joseph of the Gospels is no shrinking violet. Although the New Testament does not place any words on his lips, some careful attention will show that Joseph is a full, rounded character, with a real personality playing a highly developed role. In the crib, Joseph is usually located close to the manger, kneeling in rapt devotion, but we should not overlook the fact that this is a man mid-way between a crisis and an emergency.

The crisis, of course, had begun with the news that Mary was expecting a baby. Matthew's Gospel tells us that Mary 'was found to be with child from the Holy Spirit'. This expression has the potential to be slightly misleading. Yes, Mary was found to be pregnant; this was, after all, a matter of simple observation. But the fact that the pregnancy resulted from the action of the Holy

Spirit was not observable. We, the readers of the Gospel, know what has happened, but Joseph does not. Upon hearing the news of Mary's pregnancy, the natural assumption for him to make is that Mary's pregnancy has occurred in accordance with nature, and this assumption plunges him into a painful crisis.

Mary's irregular pregnancy – for such indeed it was – was an affront to something more than a what-will-the-neighbours-think, small-town respectability. In order to have a sense of what was at stake, we need to be aware of prevailing Jewish custom with regard to betrothal and marriage. Marriage was a two-step process: first, the couple took a public commitment in the presence of witnesses, and subsequently, the groom took the bride to his home, with great ceremony and festivity. A lengthy period could elapse between betrothal and the marriage ceremony, during which time the bride remained in her family home, under the guardianship of her father. For either party to be sexually involved with another person between the public commitment and the completed marriage was considered adultery; and in the case of the woman, adultery – at least in principle – carried a penalty of death by stoning.

This is the background to the shock felt by Joseph on hearing of Mary's pregnancy. From his perspective, the natural conclusion to be drawn was that his betrothed had engaged in an adulterous liaison, one which not only brought shame upon all concerned, but which could place Mary's very life in danger. The Gospel makes but a brief and understated reference to Joseph's turmoil upon hearing Mary's news: 'Her husband Joseph, being a righteous man and unwilling to expose her to public disgrace, planned to dismiss her quietly' (Mt 1:19). Joseph could have nothing more to do with Mary. Yet he would not shame or denounce her; to the contrary, he would actively seek to shield her from public opprobrium. But he could no longer consider taking her as his bride. Justice must be done, and justice meant cutting Mary out of his life.

When the Gospel tells us that Joseph was a just, or righteous, man, it does not mean simply that he was kindly, decent, honest, or gentle. In the Jewish religion, righteousness had the very precise meaning of adherence to religious law. It was precisely as a righteous man that Joseph would have to dismiss Mary, and this was at the heart of his crisis. As a devout Jew, he desired to keep the law fully, yet keeping the law fully would mean exposing his apparently unfaithful fiancée to the full rigour of the law. However, Joseph also wished to act with compassion. Could he shield Mary from suffering, while also acting in accordance with his deeply held convictions? In the event, Joseph resolved to act in accordance with the law, but to mitigate the likely consequences for Mary by keeping the matter secret.

Joseph's inner turmoil will, of course, be resolved shortly by the angel's explanation that Mary's child is from the Holy Spirit. The impression given by the Gospel is that Joseph's crisis is brief, but brevity does not rule out intensity. Biblically speaking, there is something almost God-like about the struggle between Joseph's righteousness and his compassion. The prophet Hosea (11:8) conveys the crisis in the heart of God, precipitated by the conflict between his compassion and the real need to address the infidelity of his people: 'How can I give you up, Ephraim? How can I hand you over, O Israel? How can I make you like Admah? How can I treat you like Zeboiim? My heart recoils within me; my compassion grows warm and tender.' Joseph, called to foster the Son of God, is being formed in the Father's likeness in the crucible of crisis.

The divine timing is very exact. Just as Joseph has decided to divorce Mary in secret, an angel reassures him in a dream, and his anxieties are laid to rest. It is God's own word, spoken through the angel, that finally and fully resolves the crisis. Joseph's initial attempt to resolve the matter had been based on purely human perception, on limited human understanding. Now that God has spoken, now that his word has been received by a just man, the divine plan can continue unfolding.

Joseph's part in this plan is nothing short of immense, and his stature is indicated by the manner in which the angel addresses him: 'Joseph, Son of David' (Mt 1:20). Matthew's Gospel opens with the words, 'An account of the genealogy of Jesus the Messiah, the son of David, the son of Abraham.' The title 'Son of David' is used several times in the Gospel, and it is reserved to Jesus, with the unique exception of Joseph. In fact it is through Joseph that Jesus receives this title; it is through Joseph that Jesus is incorporated into the royal house of David and takes his place in Israel's kingly line. Jesus will be considered the son of David precisely because Joseph has taken Mary to be his wife, and has himself named her son, Jesus, in keeping with the angel's instruction. Finally, even the structure of Matthew's Gospel underlines the importance of Joseph: the two passages in which Joseph figures prominently (Mt 1:18-25; 2:3-23), form a framework around the story of Jesus' birth and the visit of the wise men.

When Joseph awoke from the dream in which the angel had appeared to him, he did exactly what he had been asked: setting aside his plan to dismiss Mary in secret, he took her as his wife, and once the child was born, Joseph named him Jesus. The deepest nature of Joseph's righteousness is seen not in external compliance with laws and customs, but in his inner attitude of complete receptivity to God's word. What Mary said explicitly, Joseph's actions say implicitly: 'Your word be done to me.' In this matter, we can say that Joseph and Mary were well matched.

Joseph's righteousness is not a hard, unyielding attitude; rather, the quality he shows is one that is made gentle by compassion. This righteousness without rigidity is a truer reflection of God's goodness than any mere brittle religious certainty. Joseph anticipates the attitude Jesus would call for later in the Gospel when he cautioned, 'unless your righteousness exceeds that of the scribes and Pharisees, you will never enter the kingdom of heaven' (Mt 5:20). Jesus spoke those words during his 'Sermon on the Mount', and in his conclusion to that sermon he said: 'Everyone who hears these words of mine and acts on them will be like a wise man who built his house on rock. The rain fell, the floods came, and the winds blew and beat on that house, but it did not fall, because it had been founded on rock' (Mt 7:24-25). These words can apply perfectly to Joseph, whose obedience to God's word is itself word-perfect. The Gospel, in fact, takes great care to stress Joseph's commitment to carrying out God's word: during the story of the journeys to and from Egypt, we read twice how Joseph's actions are a word-for-word repetition of the command he has received from the angel (Mt 2:13-14; 20-21). If, as the adult Jesus would tell his followers, obedience to his word is the only reliable foundation on which to build, it is clear that Joseph anticipated this wisdom, by offering his complete and free assent to God's word. In effect, Joseph's obedience is the foundation on which God builds a home for his son.

From what we have seen, it follows that Joseph is no insipid plaster saint, but a robust and determined man who successfully navigates his way through both crisis and emergency. The serenity of the figures in the crib might lead us to forget that a dire emergency is imminent, the response to which will place Joseph once again at centre stage. Herod, furious that the wise men have left the region without revealing the location of the newborn Jesus, is determined to eliminate the threat by means of a general execution of infant boys. Jesus, too, is at risk, and an angel once again speaks to Joseph in a dream, warning him to flee to Egypt with the child and his mother. Joseph undertakes the journey to Egypt at night, under the cover of darkness, so providing us with another example of the irony we occasionally encounter in the Gospel. As a rule, it is evil that seeks the cover of darkness. Jesus himself adverts to this: 'For all who do evil hate the light and do not come to the light, so that their deeds may not be exposed, but those who do what is true come to the light' (Jn 3:20-21). But now Joseph, a truly good and just man, must avoid the light and seek out the cover of darkness.

There is a time, an hour, when darkness prevails, when light appears to have been vanquished, when sin and suffering seem poised for victory. The hour in which Herod slaughtered the innocents was one such time. Jesus' passion was 'the hour' which he had predicted, for which he had come into the world. In the Gospel accounts of Jesus' passion, the word 'hour' virtually becomes a technical term, used to refer specifically to that time when the power of evil has the upper hand. Jesus prays that he may be saved from this hour (Jn 12:27); to those who come to arrest him, Jesus says, 'This is your hour, and the power of darkness'. In his Sermon on the Mount, Jesus urged his followers: 'You are the light of the world ... let your light shine before others, so that they may see your good works and give glory to your Father in heaven' (Mt 5:14; 16). For now, however, the light of Joseph, this just and obedient man, must remain hidden, as he and his family flee like hunted criminals.

In Matthew's recounting of the birth of Jesus, the two principal parts are played by Herod and Joseph. While these two men are as dissimilar as light and darkness, as the story unfolds, they have some points in common. To both of these men, the initial report regarding Jesus is disturbing, and both of them have recourse to an element of secrecy in how they react to that news. Joseph, as we have seen, is troubled to hear of Mary's pregnancy. But his is not the fear and anger of a man bent on self-preservation; even before the angel's message, he is intent on protecting Mary by acting secretly. Then, when the truth about Jesus is pointed out to him, Joseph does not cling conceitedly to his earlier understanding, but opens himself fully to God's plan. Herod, in contrast, on hearing the newborn child described as king of the Jews, summons the wise men secretly so that he can eliminate the perceived threat to his rule. In Herod, there is not a hint of openness, or of willingness to consider his position.

Herod is a man who knows his own mind, and not even God will alter his outlook. While Joseph shows us that there can be much to be said for a change of mind, Herod shows the evil that can result when human frailty is clad in the armour of certainty.

Wordlessly, the person of Joseph teaches us an important lesson about Jesus, a lesson we learn by turning to the very earliest books of the Bible. In the book of Genesis (chapter 37), another Joseph, the son of Israel, is a man gifted with vivid dreams. Because he is particularly favoured by his father, Joseph incurs the jealousy of his brothers, who sell him as a slave to some traders who bring him to Egypt. Some time later, Joseph's brothers travel to Egypt in order to escape from a famine at home. There, they find that Joseph has risen to the position of prime minister, and after a reconciliation with their brother, all the children of Israel settle in Egypt. Many years later, the descendants of Israel fall out of favour with Pharaoh, the king of Egypt. The beginning of the Book of Exodus describes how one child, Moses, is secretly kept safe during Pharaoh's mass murder of infant Hebrew boys, and how he goes on to lead the descendants of Israel out of their captivity.

Two Josephs, two descents into Egypt, two rulers bent on eliminating infants whom they perceive to be a threat; two children spared. One child is Moses, who grows up to lead his people from slavery to a hostile power. The other is Jesus, who will grow up to lead all people to freedom from the power of sin and death. In our crib, the presence of the silent Joseph speaks volumes about the identity and mission of Jesus. The child beside whom Joseph kneels is the new Moses. He will not wander in the desert for forty years, along with the people of Israel who will later cross the river Jordan into the promised land. Instead, the new Moses will be tempted in the desert for forty days, before crossing back over the Jordan to call a new people to himself.

Joseph reminds us that Jesus is our deliverer; the one who, if we open our hearts to him, will lead us from every captivity to the fullness of freedom. Joseph points to the truth about Jesus, silently anticipating the words Jesus would later speak to his followers: 'You will know the truth, and the truth will make you free' (Jn 8:32).

Joseph, guardian of Jesus and husband of Mary, fades without fanfare from the pages of Matthew's Gospel. He is referred to once again in Luke's Gospel, when the twelve-year-old Jesus goes missing for three days before being found in the Temple in Jerusalem. At the end of that incident, we read that Jesus returned to Nazareth and was obedient to Mary and Joseph. Joseph is conspicuous by his absence from the story of the passion, especially where Jesus, as he dies on the cross, entrusts Mary to the care of John the disciple (Jn 19:26-27). From this episode, we can conclude that Joseph has already died. It is reasonable to draw a further conclusion: that Joseph had died in the company of Jesus and Mary. For this reason, Joseph is honoured as the patron saint of the dying. He is the 'good and faithful servant' (Mt 25:23), whose humble and selfless dedication remain a model, an inspiration and a hope.

Points to ponder

+ Joseph, patron saint of the dying, can also be considered
  the patron of those who struggle to live by their faith
  commitments, those who seek to be guided by both truth and
  compassion. He is the model for believers who reject both
  a vague, truthless compassion and a harsh, compassionless
  truth. The experience of an apparently irresolvable conflict
  between the demands of truth and the demands of love
  is not a modern conundrum, but one which Joseph felt
  with great intensity. For this reason, the silent Joseph can
  speak eloquently to those who grieve over loved ones who
  appear to be straying, and to those whose relationships are

fraught and difficult. His example can remind us that while tensions may be very real indeed, neither love nor truth need be abandoned: we can have both; we are intended to live by both – to live the truth in love, and to love in the truth. Equally, Joseph reminds us that the path we must walk is at times difficult and precarious. Those who aspire to both loving fidelity and faithful love will experience moments of tension, confusion and doubt. Such moments arise from our frail human nature, and they are compounded by our contemporary culture, which drives a wedge between love and truth. In Joseph, the righteous and loving spouse of the mother of Jesus, we find both truth and love in abundance.

✢ Obedience to the word of God is hospitality to Jesus! Joseph, we have seen, is the man who builds on the solid foundation which is hearing and acting upon the word. In so doing, Joseph builds a home for the incarnate word, Jesus himself. To be a believer is to be called to the hospitality of obedience. It is unfortunate that the word 'obedience' often carries negative overtones, that it is construed as a clipping of the disciple's wings, whereas in reality, those who generously receive God's word take flight! Even in human terms, they reap a harvest, 'Yielding thirty and sixty and a hundredfold' (Mk 4:8). Joseph brings life and warmth to the notion of obedience by inviting us to think of it as hospitality rather than as mere submissiveness.

✢ 'Your word is a lamp to my feet and a light to my path.' These words from Psalm 119 (verse 105) both reassure and caution us: when we accept God's guidance, we will not go astray; when we follow our own way, independently of the light of God's wisdom, we risk stumbling. Aside from God's word, our understanding is limited and partial. Our minds need to be purified and illuminated by a wisdom greater than our own, just as Joseph's understanding was expanded by the angel's message. Jesus tells us that we are cleansed, pruned, purified by his word (Jn 15:3). Occasionally, it may seem that our hospitality is extended to a demanding guest, but it is when God's word is at its most challenging that it can work the greatest transformation within us.

Chapter Eight

Woman of Vulnerability and Strength: Mary, the Mother of Jesus

> ... to bear in her womb
> Infinite weight and lightness; to carry
> in hidden, finite inwardness,
> nine months of Eternity; to contain
> in slender vase of being,
> the sum of power –
> in narrow flesh,
> the sum of light.
>   Then bring to birth,
> push out into air, a Man-child
> needing, like any other,
> milk and love –
> but who was God.
>   Denise Levertov (1923–1997), 'Annunciation'

In the opening chapter, we saw that a particular blessing the crib offers is its capacity to re-enchant, to open our hearts anew to a sense of mystery and wonder. We noted that this is not about escapism, but openness to the heart of reality. The blessing of re-enchantment therefore includes a challenge: we are challenged to move beyond mere sentimentality, and to hear what the message of Christmas has to say to the rough edges of our experience, to the rawness of our humanity. We live in a world of both light and shade. Our Christian faith is not about fleeing the latter in favour of the former; it is about how God's grace comes to penetrate everywhere. The sheer delightfulness of the crib-scene can be construed – or rather, misconstrued – as an invitation to indulge in some saccharine sentimentality, as a welcome break from life's harshness. Let us not for a moment downplay the delight and the wonder of Christmas; but properly understood, the crib sends us back to the heart of reality with renewed hope, renewed vision and a renewed capacity to bear life's burdens.

The risk of remaining at the level of sentiment is perhaps greatest in our contemplation of Mary and Jesus. Yet the infant Jesus comes armed with something akin to religious dynamite. He has aroused the wrath of Herod and has usurped titles belonging to Caesar. He has, he will tell his followers in due time, come to cast fire upon the earth (Lk 12:49). But for now, let us give our attention to Mary. We are, perhaps, so accustomed to thinking of Mary as gentle that we fail to consider her great strength. We may even fall into the error of considering gentleness and strength to be opposites, mutually exclusive qualities. Nothing, however, could be further from the truth: at times it can take great strength to be gentle, and there are times when the proper exercise of strength calls for great gentleness. Mary the mother of Jesus, the first disciple, shows us gentleness and strength working together rather than being in tension with each other. Her gentleness is evident, but she is also the woman of strength, the *mulier fortis*.

Mary is present in the crib, indeed the crib itself exists because she gave her 'yes' to God's plan. Mary lived in a close-knit community, held together by strict religious values. The angel Gabriel gave her no reason to assume that the rest of the community would react well to the news of her pregnancy. Certainly he reassured Mary, but he did not go into any detail regarding how God's plan was to unfold. People talk; they talk now and they talked then, and words can be hurtful and bewildering. For this reason alone, Mary's 'yes' revealed uncommon strength and courage.

This young woman kneeling beside the manger in the crib has given her consent to God. As we contemplate her, next to her infant son, the ramifications of her consent are only just beginning to make themselves felt. That 'yes' pronounced nine months earlier in her home in Nazareth has begun to draw upon her reserves of faith, trust and generosity. Happily, it had been a robust 'yes', based on genuine inner strength, rather than on a simple desire to please – which can be a sign of weakness. Recall that when the angel Gabriel told Mary that she would conceive Jesus, she did not ask: 'What will the neighbours think', but, 'How can this be?' Mary had not been pressurised or intimidated by the mighty angelic visitor. Her question showed a marvellous degree of self-possession, and precisely because she was self-possessed, because she had ownership of herself, Mary was fully free to give herself away; to give herself to God, by entering into his plan and setting aside any plans she may have had.

Mary's great 'yes', the 'yes' which brought Jesus into the world, was based not on understanding, but on faith and trust. When, as happened at various times during the life of her son, that 'yes' was put to the test, it was renewed not by further information from an angelic visitor, but by courageous fidelity. We can say that in a sense, once Mary had given her consent, she was left on her own. There was no ongoing reassurance, no cloud by day or flame by night, no further annunciation, no heavenly commentary as events unfolded. Mary was left in the stark silence of faith. Luke's Gospel makes all of this utterly clear, by telling us bluntly that once Mary had agreed to become the mother of Jesus, 'the angel departed from her'. Once she had accepted God's word, God took Mary at her word. It is in the nature of adult faith that God's apparent absence is in fact his acceptance of our consent. It is in his silence that God underwrites our words of commitment to his plan. Disciples help to move this plan forward not by proof and understanding, but by faith and trust.

Did Mary's consent to become the mother of Jesus leave her, then, in a position of passivity? Did her obedience entail the surrender of some of her humanity? Having possessed herself so fully, in giving herself, did she give herself away? Such questions are worth considering, since they touch on the nature of discipleship, and they can help to expose some fundamental misunderstandings regarding the relationship between our human freedom and our faith commitment. Some portrayals of Mary tend to suggest that she was passive in her obedience, or that her femininity was of a 'traditional' passive kind. The truth of the matter is that in Mary there is both passivity and activity, and this applies to every Christian. Let us look first at Mary's passivity, conscious that the very concept is mistrusted by the culture we inhabit.

Every Christian vocation is passive in its origins. Whether we consider the foundational vocation of baptism, or a particular call to a particular task, no individual calls herself or himself. A vocation, or calling, is just that: a calling. And it is in the nature of a calling that it comes from outside of oneself – it is received, accepted, consented to. From the perspective of a helpless infant, baptism is entirely passive. The infant plays no role other than being present. This does not entail any violence to the infant, nor does it mean he or she is 'reduced' to a state of passivity. Rather, it means that for the infant, baptism is pure gift, utterly unmerited. The little one is – passively – caught up in God's loving plan. This moment of passivity is found at the beginning of every call, including the call of Mary to be the mother of Jesus. Mary neither invited nor expected the angel. To this extent, she was truly passive; the call she received involved no initiative of her own.

But that was where Mary's passivity ended. Once the invitation was extended, she engaged actively with it, not hesitating even to express her incomprehension. God's call, passively received, must be actively assented to, and there is an enormous contrast between the unanticipated nature of the angel's visit to Mary in Nazareth, and the careful, deliberate quality of her consent to the angel's invitation. Furthermore, while Mary's consent to God's plan might well have obliged her to relinquish other hopes or dreams for her life, it did not prevent her from taking the initiative, and making further plans of her own. Shortly after the angel's visit, Mary set off to visit her cousin, Elizabeth, in the Judaean hills. We do not know with certainty where Elizabeth lived, but the region referred to in the Gospel was sixty kilometres south of Nazareth. This was not a journey to be undertaken lightly – and on foot – by anyone playing a role of delicate passivity!

From the details given to us by the Gospel, we can say that Mary's visit to Elizabeth had a threefold purpose: it would enable Mary to rejoice with Elizabeth in the good news of her older cousin's pregnancy, and in so doing deepen her own sense of the reality of God's action; it would enable Mary to offer practical help to Elizabeth, who was now in her sixth month; most importantly, the visit would enable Mary to share the marvellous news of what God was doing in her. Mary's sustained song of praise, spoken in the presence of Elizabeth, suggests that the third of these reasons was the most pressing one: having given her consent to God's plan, Mary could not contain her delight and excitement, but simply had to share the good news with others, starting with her cousin.

Mary's sharing with Elizabeth was spontaneous and un-restrained, and sooner or later she would have to communicate the news of her pregnancy to others. Not everyone would be as well disposed as Mary's cousin, for whom her own pregnancy was already a sign of the wonderful things God was doing. When and how would Mary tell her family in Nazareth? Whom would she tell first? How would Joseph be informed? The Gospel does not satisfy curiosity regarding such details, but one thing is sure: the reality Mary was to face on her return from Elizabeth's home called for courage and strength.

We typically, and rightly, acclaim Mary's humility, yet this was an attitude that co-existed with the conviction that God was doing great things in her. In Mary, there was neither conflict nor contradiction between her humility and the belief that she was greatly blessed. Moreover, Mary was convinced that she would be permanently acclaimed as blessed; she openly expressed this to Elizabeth: 'Surely, from now on all generations will call me blessed' (Lk 1:48). There is not the faintest hint of false modesty or self-effacement here, not for a moment would Mary deny that she had been blessed, since the glory belonged to God and God deserved full credit. In saying: 'My soul magnifies the Lord' (Lk 1:46), Mary anticipates what Saint Paul, quoting the prophet Jeremiah, would later say about boasting: 'Let the one who boasts, boast in the Lord' (1 Cor 1:31). In Mary, we see that to be a committed servant of the Lord is not to be subservient, but to experience a new intensity and depth of life, even here and now. Whereas we sometimes fear that a more committed 'yes' to God will curtail and truncate us, Mary's 'yes' expanded her personality rather than limited it.

In telling the story of Jesus' birth, the Gospel of Matthew focuses most strongly on Joseph, while Luke gives greater prominence to Mary. Careful attention to the role of women is a distinctive feature of Luke's Gospel. He is, for example, the only one of the evangelists to mention Elizabeth, or Anna the elderly prophetess in the Temple (Lk 2:36-38). Only Luke describes in any detail the visit of Jesus to the home of Martha and Mary (Lk 10:38-42), and only in Luke do we read that Jesus was given financial help by a small group of women (Lk 8:1-3). These details are highly significant when we bear in mind that in the strongly patriarchal culture of the time, women tended to be marginal at best. Luke brings women in from the margins, highlighting their role in God's unfolding plan. The words of

Mary in her hymn of praise, 'He has looked with favour on the lowliness of his servant', could be applied more generally to the women in Luke's Gospel. While it would be anachronistic to regard either Luke or his portrayal of Mary as feminist, an important precedent is set for the role of women in the origins of our Christian faith.

If, on returning from her visit to Elizabeth, Mary had made any particular plans around her pregnancy, they were scuttled not by God but by Caesar. According to Luke's Gospel, the census ordered by the emperor Augustus took Mary away from the familiarity of home at the very time when it would have been most comforting. And since the crowds in Bethlehem for the census seem to have made it impossible to secure decent accommodation, Mary, having given birth under extremely unsuitable conditions, had to place her newborn child in a manger, a feeding trough. The face of Mary on the statue in our crib could realistically be lined with care and exhaustion. Devotion, yes. Wonder and delight, without doubt. But the circumstances of her child's birth cannot have been anything other than immensely trying.

After telling us that she laid her child in a manger, the next thing Luke's Gospel tells us about Mary is that she 'treasured all these words and pondered them in her heart' (Lk 2:19). Luke's Greek is better translated to read that Mary treasured all these things, or events. But just what was it that Mary treasured and pondered? Most immediately, the Gospel refers to the visit of the shepherds, who had conveyed what the angel had said about Jesus. The sudden appearance of a group of simple men, sharing the message that the infant in the manger was Saviour, Messiah and Lord (Lk 2:11), must have touched Mary very deeply. Not even the angel Gabriel had used these titles in relation to the child Mary was to bear. Granted, Elizabeth had welcomed Mary as 'the mother of my Lord', but now, in remarkably humble circumstances, the identity of Jesus is confirmed by the shepherds. Their message is something to be dwelt on at length, to be treasured and pondered.

There was, of course, more than sweetness and light to be considered. Luke's language suggests that Mary pondered not just the visit of the shepherds, but the overall circumstances of Jesus' birth. By this stage, there was much to ponder: the visit of the angel and his extraordinary promise; the visit to Elizabeth, during which the two expectant mothers shared their delight in God's ways; the upheaval and stress of the journey from Nazareth to Bethlehem; the realisation that the child was about to be born; the failure to find accommodation suitable for childbirth; the bizarre inconsistency between giving birth to one described as the 'Son of God' and having to place him in a manger. Then, finally, the visit of the shepherds, outsiders, whose presence seemed calculated to assure Mary that God was at work in all these things. Yes, there was indeed much to ponder!

A glance ahead in Luke's Gospel, to the end of the episode when Mary and Joseph found the boy Jesus in the Temple (Lk 2:51), shows once again that Mary treasured those things in her heart. At this point, to her list of things to ponder, Mary can add the strange precociousness of Jesus, who had sat among the religious scholars of the Temple and shared in their discussion. Jesus' reply to his mother's gentle rebuke gave Mary further food for thought: 'Did you not know that I must be in my Father's house?' This singularly independent child was asserting himself at a young age.

Christian tradition regards Mary as the great contemplative. To contemplate means to look, to regard deeply, steadily and reflectively. The Gospel's references to Mary's thoughts suggest that she began her contemplative career early. We can imagine the various ways in which she looked at the unfolding mystery that was the life of her son. At the moment of the annunciation, when she learned of God's plan, Mary's attention will have been focused inwards. She has not seen Jesus yet, but her mind is being given more and more to God's will and his purpose. At his birth, Mary will have regarded Jesus with love, pure and simple, and it is this moment of contemplation that the figure in the crib is most often intended to capture. Some years later, when the pre-teenage Jesus was asserting his independence in the Temple, Mary's regard was one of questioning concern: 'Child, why have you treated us like this?' At the wedding feast of Cana, recounted in chapter two of John's Gospel, Mary contemplated Jesus with an enormous depth of understanding. On that occasion, as she looked at her son, she fully expected him to do great things. Later still, as Jesus hung helplessly upon the cross, Mary contemplated him with a sorrow that defies description. After the resurrection, Mary will have beheld her son with transcendent astonishment and glory.

Mary's contemplation of Jesus was in the marrow of her bones. It more than mirrors the moments of delight and despair that are part and parcel of human relationships. As we contemplate the great contemplative in the crib at Christmas, we can reflect that at that moment, the serene Mary had a long and arduous path of discipleship ahead of her. As we offer her our praise and petitions, we can be encouraged on our own pilgrimage by her example of strength and fidelity.

Points to ponder

+ Mary, we have seen, lived by faith and not by sight. Is it not unfair that as soon as Mary had given her consent, her 'yes' to God's word, she was left on her own? Given the role Mary was to play in God's plan, we might have expected things to be different. Surely some abiding token of God's presence would have been in order, at least until her pregnancy become evident? Something of the pattern of Mary's experience can regularly be seen in the lives of those who seek to live by God's word. Let us say, for example, that a sincere Christian prays for the gift of stronger faith and trust, only to feel within a short while that they have less of these than ever. Indeed, it often seems that God withdraws from people just as they determine to commit themselves more deeply to him. The experience of Mary would suggest that God's apparent absence means that he is taking his servants at their word. It is as though God were saying, 'My dear child, do you want to grow in faith and trust? Then I will give you the opportunity to practice them. There's no better time for you to practice faith and trust than when I seem to be absent, and so I will now allow you to feel that I am absent!' Faith and trust are not a feeling that God is close to hand. The reality is almost the opposite: faith and trust are what sustains us just when our feelings would tell us that God is very silent and very far away. God's silence can at times seem virtually scandalous, and believers may experience times of genuine anguish. However, in our day-to-day discipleship, Mary invites us not to fear the Father's silence, but to receive it gladly, as an expression of his loving pedagogy.

+ In his first letter to the Corinthians (9:16), Saint Paul writes, 'Woe to me if I do not proclaim the gospel!' It is not that Paul fears some external punishment if he fails to proclaim the good news. Rather, he is so taken up with what God has done in Jesus that he is 'bursting' to tell people. Having received the good news himself, Paul cannot hold it in. The same is true of Mary as she hurries to visit her cousin Elizabeth. Good news must be shared. The Gospel is not a secret; it is intended to be proclaimed from the rooftops (Lk 12:3). The exuberance of Paul's 'Woe to me if I do not proclaim' and the enthusiasm of Mary's hasty departure to the hill country of Judah raise questions for every believer. How have I been blessed by the gift of faith? What have I received that I would wish for my loved ones and for the entire world? How might

I, in my own way and in my own circumstances, share the blessing? If the news of Christ really is good news, then it should not need the support of threats, nagging, criticism or cajoling. The best way to proclaim the good news is to be convinced by it, and to live according to our conviction. At issue here is not so much an examination of conscience in which we focus on our lukewarm responses; rather, what is required is a growing conviction that our faith is a treasure, the 'pearl of great value' (Mt 13:46). It is this conviction that makes faith contagious, and there is no better way to grow in this conviction than to consider the ways in which we have been blessed.

✛ Mary had not been expecting the shepherds – they simply turned up. The news they brought, that the child in the crib was Saviour, Messiah and Lord – was pure grace. If we set ourselves to count our blessings, one question we might ask is where we have experienced unexpected favours. Perhaps some words of encouragement we read or heard that enabled us to persevere hopefully through a time of loss or anxiety; or a chance meeting that gave us an opportunity to show compassion to someone in need; or a sudden reconciliation after a period of coolness in a relationship. God's grace can overtake us in many unexpected ways, and as we become practiced in recognising this, we can make our own the words of the book of Lamentations (3:22-23): 'The steadfast love of the Lord never ceases, his mercies never come to an end; they are new every morning; great is your faithfulness.'

Chapter Nine

The Infant in the Manger:
The Christ, the Lord, the Saviour

> But the child that is Noble and not Mild
> He lies in his cot. He is unbeguiled.
> He is Noble, he is not Mild,
> And he is born to make men wild.
>
> Stevie Smith (1902–1971), 'Christmas'

When it comes to contemplation of the crib, a sense of enchantment can be both friend and foe. Parched souls in a disenchanted world long for re-enchantment, and the crib both appeals to this longing and promises refreshment. But as we suggested at the very beginning of these reflections, the re-enchantment offered by the crib does not invite us to linger in some form of escapism; rather, it commissions us to face reality with a new vision and a new attitude. Far from sweeping us up into irrelevant romanticism, the wonder and delight of the crib scene can nourish us, equip us for the struggle that is discipleship.

The lines with which we have begun this chapter, from Stevie Smith's poem, 'Christmas', insist that there is more to the infant in the crib than 'Gentle Jesus, meek and mild'. Smith reminds us that this child is 'Born to make men wild'. Just a few weeks after his birth, the parents of Jesus will hear the elderly prophet, Simeon, announce that their infant son is 'Destined for the falling and rising of many in Israel' (Lk 2:34). This is a perplexing, uncomfortable prophecy, one that must sound worrying to the parents of the infant Jesus. Simeon underlines the wildness of the plan which is unfolding in the infant Jesus by saying to Mary, 'A sword will pierce your own soul too' (Lk 2:35). Even as we contemplate Jesus in the crib, we know that he has long since grown up to cast fire upon the earth, to begin a revolution, to make men wild.

The newborn child is our Saviour, which of course implies that there is something from which we must be saved. The stark fact of the matter is that there is tragedy at the heart of Christmas – the tragedy of human waywardness; the tragedy of sin. This means that the true joy of Christmas runs far deeper than seasonal jollity: Christmas rejoicing is rejoicing over our redemption, over what Christ has done for us. The backdrop of shadow and darkness means that Christmas can never be only a matter of enchantment, merely an indulgence in romance. These lines from G. K. Chesterton's poem, 'The Nativity', disallow any kind of infatuation with the romance and enchantment of Christmas:

> Have a myriad children been quickened,
> Have a myriad children grown old,
> Grown gross and unloved and embittered,
> Grown cunning and savage and cold?
> God abides in a terrible patience,
> Unangered, unworn,
> And again for the child that was squandered
> A child is born.

To a humanity that has squandered its childhood and lost its innocence, God has sent an innocent child, his son. This child will grow up to take upon himself the bitterness, savagery and coldness of our race. He will offer no resistance, but forever prove that self-giving love is the better way, the stronger way. He will absorb every offence that humanity has to offer, and he will overcome. He will overcome simply because love is stronger than hatred, stronger even than death. And having overcome, he will open a new way for humanity: the way of reconciliation and of peace. This victory gained by Jesus, a victory achieved over tragedy and through tragedy, was what lay ahead of the newborn Jesus as he was tenderly placed in the manger. It is what gives meaning to our attitude of reverence and thanksgiving, as we contemplate the child in the crib.

In our efforts to learn and live our faith, images can be of enormous help to us. Frescoes, mosaics, statues and icons capture something of the reality of God. Likewise, the Christmas crib is far more than an illustration: it can help to draw us into God's plan. Yet there is infinitely more to what God is about than any image or representation can ever capture. Jesus himself is the only entirely adequate representation of God. He himself said to the apostle Thomas, 'Whoever has seen me has seen the Father' (Jn 14:9). But not even our best representations can come close to capturing the full reality of Jesus, and as we contemplate the crib, it is good to bear in mind that it is our privilege to bow, with open hearts and open minds, before a mystery that is too great for our hearts and minds to accommodate. Through the centuries, many saints and scholars have taken care to insist that our images and representations, helpful though they may be, can never fully capture the reality of God. To the extent that we expect them to, they can actually begin to obscure rather than illuminate. The risk of placing too much confidence in images is eloquently conveyed by Rainer Maria Rilke, in his poem 'We must not portray you in king's robes':

> Piously we produce our images of you
> till they stand around you like a thousand walls.
> And when our hearts would simply open,
> our fervent hands hide you.

The crib does not so much unveil the mystery of Jesus as draw us into the mystery, helping us to sense how God's plan is working out in our own lives, our own darkness and light, suffering and joy. The best attitude to bring to our contemplation of the child in the manger is one of empty-handedness, of receptivity. We are not the visitors from the East, bringing treasures and wisdom; the most realistic things we can lay before the Christ-child are our poverty, our struggles and our loving gratitude.

In Luke's Gospel, we read that Mary wrapped Jesus in swaddling clothes before placing him in the manger. Wrapping newborn children in bands of cloth was a common practice, intended to strengthen and support their frail bodies. Now, the source of all strength, the Saviour of the world, needs the support of bands of cloth; he has become a helpless infant, dependant on others for his every need. It may also be that the reference to swaddling clothes is intended to echo an obscure verse from the Old Testament. In the book of Wisdom (7:4-5), King Solomon says, 'I was nursed with care in swaddling cloths. For no king has had a different beginning of existence'. In Jesus, the Son of God now shares the lot of all people, commoners and kings alike. If there is any respect in which the beginning of his earthly existence stands out, it is in the humility of the circumstances.

The prologue of the Gospel of John says of Jesus, 'He came to what was his own, and his own people did not accept him' (Jn 1:11). This brief, ominous note at the beginning of the Gospel anticipates the rejection of Jesus by his peers and by the religious and political leaders of his time. Luke's Gospel makes the same point in a more prosaic way, by letting us know that there was no room for Jesus and his family at the inn (Lk 2:7). Rejection is the lot of this child, and even as we offer homage to the newborn king, we do well to bear in mind the Old Testament prophecy which was applied to Jesus by some of his earliest followers, 'He was despised and rejected by others; a man of suffering and acquainted with infirmity' (Isa 53:3).

Do these notes of realism, this repeated insistence on the human frailty and humility of Jesus, take from the joy of Christmas? Do we not, perhaps, run the risk of disenchanting precisely where we have sought to re-enchant? Nothing could be further from the truth! The most disenchanted, disenchanting and artificial Christmas is the exclusively commercial and secular mutant. Wall-to-wall glitter and unceasing 'seasonal' music simply fail to connect with a large and unavoidable element of the human situation: the reality of suffering. But the child in the manger will drink the cup of human suffering to its dregs. We need not lament the kind of 'Christmas' that gets swept away on a tide of tinsel, nor bleat about 'putting Christ back into Christmas'. Christ has never been removed from Christmas! What has happened is that some celebrations that coincide with the season of Christmas have been far removed from Christ; have no trace of him, no inkling of what God has done and is doing for his people. We do no service to the authenticity of Christmas by standing in po-faced judgment over the world's desperate search for happiness. The challenge to believers is to live an authentic life, a life that might awaken in others a desire for God, the source of true and lasting happiness.

'The Word became flesh and lived among us' (Jn 1:14). This is the sole allusion that the Gospel of John makes to the event of Christmas. It was at the first Christmas that Jesus, the Word, was born in human flesh and began to live among people. But Jesus was the Word of God before he took on human flesh; the opening line of John's Gospel reads: 'In the beginning was the Word, and the Word was with God, and the Word was God.' In calling Jesus 'the Word', the Gospel tells us that God has nothing more to say than he has said in Jesus: Jesus, the first Word, the Word who was present from the beginning, is also God's last word. The letter to the Hebrews spells out the fact that in Jesus, God really has said everything he has to say; it opens by recalling the fact that down through history, God has spoken in various ways by the prophets, but that now, 'he has spoken to us by a Son' (Heb 1:2).

This is who Jesus is: God's definitive word, everything that needs to be said to men and women. Yet now, God's first and last Word is a wordless infant lying in a manger! Some artistic representations of the nativity depict the infant Jesus sitting on his Mother's knee, in full command of all he surveys, knowingly imparting blessings to his visitors. But this is not the Jesus of the Gospel, and such depictions – whatever their theological intention – are blind to the humility of God, a humility that is real rather than merely apparent. The infant in the manger is a real infant, not a wise teacher in an infant's body. He will soon be a wise teacher, but at the first Christmas, Jesus is an infant through and through. In due time, the Word of God will begin his public ministry with the prophetic words: 'The time is fulfilled, and the kingdom of God has come near; repent, and believe in the good news' (Mk 1:15). But the visitors to the stable at Bethlehem do not hear a prophet; they encounter only the disarming charm of an infant. The incarnate Word has yet to speak his first words.

The child in the crib is, as the angels have proclaimed, Saviour, Messiah and Lord. He is these things in fullness, even as an infant in the crib. Yet in a very real sense, Jesus is an apprentice: he has things to learn, things to experience and things to suffer. Hebrews puts it very plainly, in telling us that although Jesus was God's son, 'He learned obedience through what he suffered; and having been made perfect, he became the source of eternal salvation for all who obey him' (Heb 5:8-9). Whatever we may have been taught, whatever impressions certain types of piety may have conveyed, whatever the exaggerations of some kinds of religious art, it is a basic fact of our faith that Jesus is completely and utterly human. The infant of Bethlehem is just that: an infant. Reflecting on the humanity of Jesus, Hebrews tells us: 'We do not have a high priest who is unable to sympathise with our weaknesses, but we have one who in every respect has been tested as we are, yet without sin' (Heb 4:15). Jesus' complete sharing in our humanity will lead him to drink the cup of suffering to the dregs, to the point of feeling abandoned by God as he hangs on the cross, moments before his death (Mk 15:34). His sharing in our humanity is no less real at the beginning of his earthly life.

We can never adequately express the strange and terrible contrast between the innocence of the crib and the ignominy of the cross; the sweetness of the newborn child and the savagery of the fate that he will accept out of love for us. The mystery is ineffable, and when we come to the crib, whether our hearts are filled with joy or emptied by sorrow, our task is gratitude and trust. The child is real; he is God's word, spoken to the reality of our humanity; he is God's promise and God's presence.

No less striking than the contrast between the crib and the cross is the contrast between the humble state of the infant in the crib, and the fact that he is the son of God Most High. The Gospel of Mark begins with the words: 'The beginning of the good news of Jesus Christ, the Son of God.' Near the end of that Gospel, just after Jesus dies on the cross, a Roman centurion spontaneously recognises what has been proclaimed at the opening of the Gospel: 'Truly this man was God's son' (Mk 15:39). As God's son, Jesus' entire ministry and mission is to show the face of God to men and women, so much so that in Jesus, the contrast between God's humility and his majesty dissolves in paradox. This paradox is wonderfully captured in these lines from the Christmas hymn, 'Afar From Where the Sun doth Rise':

> Fast doth he sleep, where straw doth spread
> A humble manger for his bed;
> A Mother's milk that strength renewed
> Which gives the birds of heaven their food.

A key element of Jesus' humanity is his complete dependence on his mother. God's plan to send his son into the world depended from the beginning on the consent of Mary, and so it is entirely appropriate that the newborn son should rely on Mary for all his human needs. Although it is the Gospel of Luke that pays most attention to the role and response of Mary, Matthew's Gospel underlines the closeness of the relationship between the infant Jesus and his mother. In the space of just eleven verses in the second chapter of his Gospel, Matthew refers no less than five times to 'The child and his mother'. It is almost as if the newborn Jesus is incapable of existing apart from his mother ... which is to say that he is a normal baby! The Son of God, present at creation, the one who 'gives the birds of heaven their food', is a helpless infant who depends on Mary for absolutely everything. We have been considering the crib as a place of contrasts, or apparent contrasts. Contrast need not mean conflict, nor even tension, and there is a seamless continuity between the simple directness of the crib and the mature theological reflection found in Saint Paul's letter to the Philippians. In a hymn in that letter (2:6-11), Paul presents the whole itinerary of Jesus' existence, from his identity with God, his birth 'In human likeness', his death on the cross, to his exaltation as Lord. As we pause before the crib in prayer, we acknowledge with Paul that 'At the name of Jesus every knee should bend, in heaven and on earth and under the earth, and every tongue confess that Jesus Christ is Lord, to the glory of God the Father'.

Scholars like to refer to the Gospel accounts of Jesus' birth as the 'Infancy narratives', yet the same accounts tell us virtually nothing about his infancy. When parents, relatives and friends contemplate a newborn child, they look to the future. Prominent in their minds and hearts is a question that was asked about John the Baptist at the time of his birth: 'What then will this child become?' Let us now ask this question of the child in the crib. Each of the Gospels draws out some particular aspects of Jesus' personality, life and ministry, so we shall briefly consider some of the distinctive answers given by Matthew, Mark, Luke and John to the question: 'What will the infant Jesus grow up to be?'

The child in the crib will grow up to be a great teacher. We have already seen how Matthew's Gospel portrays Jesus as a new Moses who will lead a new people to freedom from captivity. When Moses and the Israelites were in the desert, between captivity in Egypt and freedom in the Promised Land, they stopped at Mount Sinai, where they received the commandments, God's loving guidance which would enable the people to remain free, and avoid falling back into slaveries of their own making. Like Moses, Jesus teaches the people from a mountain, and three entire chapters of Matthew's Gospel (chapters 5-7) are dedicated to the Sermon on the Mount, in which Jesus refines and elaborates on the teachings of Moses, and offers detailed teaching and guidance to his followers. Devotees of the child in the crib do more than just admire him; they are disciples, learners, open to being taught by the adult Christ.

The child in the crib will grow up to suffer greatly and to be misunderstood even by his closest friends. All four Gospels describe the passion in detail, but Mark pays particular attention to the opposition and suffering Jesus endured from the beginning of his public ministry. By the beginning of Mark's second chapter, there are storm clouds gathering, signs of resentment, resistance and hatred. Just one chapter later, the religious authorities are plotting to kill Jesus. Up to this point in the Gospel, all Jesus has done is heal and teach and proclaim the coming of God's kingdom, but his enemies have made up their minds: Jesus is a threat to their fixed ideas, their established way of living and acting. His opponents are not interested in studying more closely what Jesus thinks or what he stands for; they are not interested in the truth; it does not matter to them that Jesus is a transparently good man. They are bent on destruction. Devotees of the child in the crib seek to persevere in following the adult Christ, even when this means opposition and misunderstanding.

The child in the crib will grow up to be a man of prayer. The Gospel of Luke pays a great deal of attention to how Jesus prays. It is while Jesus is praying, immediately after his baptism in the river Jordan, that the Spirit descends on him like a dove (Lk 3:21-22). It is while he is praying on the Mountain of the Transfiguration that his appearance is transformed and his disciples see his glory (Lk 9:29). Jesus prays before important moments in his life, such as the calling of the twelve apostles (Lk 6:12-13), and the first prediction of his passion (Lk 9:18-22). Of the four Gospels, it is only in Luke that Jesus' disciples ask him to teach them to pray, a request he answers by teaching them the 'Our Father' (Lk 11:1-4). Jesus instructs his followers to pray diligently, especially in times of particular suffering (Lk 21:36; 22:40), and some of his parables offer great encouragement for perseverance in prayer (Lk 11:5-8; 18:1-8). Devotees of the child in the crib take to heart the words of the adult Christ, about the need 'To pray always and not to lose heart' (Lk 18:1).

The child in the crib will grow up to show men and women what God the Father is like. John's Gospel insists that 'No one has ever seen God'. Only one person is qualified to tell us about God, and that is Jesus: 'It is God the only Son, who is close to the Father's heart, who has made him known' (Jn 1:18). In showing us what God is like, in revealing him (the word revealing means 'pulling back the veil'), Jesus does not simply communicate information about God. Jesus himself is what God is like. This is why he can say, 'For God so loved the world that he gave his only son, so that everyone who believes in him may not perish but may have eternal life' (Jn 3:16). It is because Jesus is God's son that he can do more than simply point out the truth, but can tell us, 'I am the way, and the truth, and the life' (Jn 14:6). It is for the same reason that when Philip says to him, 'Lord, show us the way to the Father', Jesus can answer, 'Whoever has seen me has seen the Father' (Jn 14:8-9). In fact, Jesus had already put the matter plainly, by saying, 'The Father and I are one' (Jn 10:30).

Devotees of the child in the crib are people of whom the adult Christ can say to his Father, 'They have believed that you sent me' (Jn 17:8).

There is more to the child in the crib than meets the eye, far more than these brief reflections can consider. There is no more apposite description of the richness of the mystery of the infant Messiah than the words with which the Gospel of John concludes: 'But there are also many other things that Jesus did; if every one of them were written down, I suppose that the world itself could not contain the books that would be written.'

Points to ponder

✛ At the time of Jesus, there was a widespread expectation that God would send his people a Messiah, a great leader who would bring political and religious freedom, and usher in an era in which God's faithful people would live lives of peaceful devotion. Jesus is the expected Messiah, but in a way it would be more accurate to think of him as the unexpected Messiah. He has come in humility rather than splendour, in obscurity rather than in glory; he will serve rather than be served, offer pardon rather than seek revenge. This silent, unexpected Messiah-in-a-manger speaks volumes about how God works. He tells us that our God is a God of surprises, a God who writes straight with crooked lines, a God whose providence is always bigger than our circumstances. The attitude the child in the crib proposes to us is trust in God, even – or better, especially – when life is opaque and mysterious. The newborn Jesus invites us to a Copernican revolution in our thinking: he is the centre of the universe, the point around which reality revolves, Emmanuel, God-with-us.

✛ We have adverted to a kind of 'Christmas' that is limited to those who have the means to enjoy it; a Christmas that is not for the lowly, the poor and the meek, but for the happy, the healthy and the well-off. The circumstances of Jesus' birth make it plain that the real Christmas is an inclusive one, embracing all, but especially those whose circumstances are in any way poor and humble. Those who grieve the loss of loved ones, those whose tables at Christmas will have an empty space that was filled in earlier years, those who struggle with illness ... such people are more, not less, qualified to enter into the spirit of Christmas.

+ Near the very end of the Bible, the heavenly Jesus explains his entire project simply and briefly: 'See, I am making all things new' (Rev 21:5). This is why Jesus was born, why he took on our human nature, why he endured misunderstanding, opposition and death: so that we might shed everything that is stale and dull, and 'walk in newness of life' (Rom 6:4). The risen, heavenly Lord promises 'a new heaven and a new earth' (Rev 21:1), but for now, as we walk upon this earth, he is our hope and our strength. Even as we contemplate the child in the crib, we can pray to the Lord of glory, 'Amen. Come, Lord Jesus!' (Rev 22:20).

Chapter Ten

The Infant's Interpreters: The Ox and the Ass, the Lamb and the Manger

> A stable was Thy Court, and when
> Men turn'd to beasts, beasts would be men.
> They were Thy courtiers; others none;
> And their poor manger was Thy throne.
>
> Henry Vaughan (1621–1695), 'The Nativity'

The crib, as we noted near the beginning of these reflections, would not be complete without the humble ox and ass, and a lamb brought along by one of the visiting shepherds; yet not a single member of this small menagerie features in the Gospel accounts of the birth of Christ. We would scarcely contemplate banishing these meek creatures from our crib, in the interest of a kind of biblical rigidity – that would indeed be a suspect kind of zeal! Happily, however, we can do far more than simply tolerate the ox, the ass and the lamb as innocuous intruders. These creatures are of profound significance; furthermore, their significance is profoundly biblical. It may be no more than coincidence, but it is certainly an interesting coincidence, that in one place in Luke's Gospel, a connection is made between ox, donkey and manger. When Jesus was challenging his ultra-orthodox opponents for their rigid approach to observing the Sabbath, he noted that on the Sabbath, they themselves would untie ox and donkey from the manger and lead them to water (Lk 13:15). On its own, this suggestive connection between the two farmyard creatures and the manger could be taken as a licence to place the ox and the ass near the manger at Christmas. However, there is a far deeper link between ox, ass and manger, and it is to be found in the Old Testament.

The book of Isaiah is one of the most important books in the Bible. The longest of all the prophetic books, it was not written by a single individual, but composed by various authors over several centuries. While the study of Isaiah's authorship and editing is complex, the reason it was written is simple, and is mentioned at the very beginning of the book: 'An ox knows its owner, and an ass its master's manger; but Israel does not know, my people have not understood' (Isa 1:3, *New American Bible*). The book of Isaiah was written because God's chosen people had gone astray. This long work of prophecy was necessary because people had forgotten where their true good lay; they had turned away from the source of life and blessing, from God himself. God responded to his people's faithlessness by raising up prophets to call them back to their senses. Jesus, whose birth we celebrate, is a prophet and more than a prophet; so much so that even the one who proclaims him, John the Baptist, is himself called 'More than a prophet' (Lk 7:26). Whereas in earlier times, God sought out his straying people by raising up a series of prophets, now he has sent his own Son to seek out the lost.

What does the presence of the ox and the ass at the beginning of the prophecy of Isaiah mean for the creatures in our crib? Quite simply, these ordinary creatures can serve as interpreters of Jesus. The child in the manger is the one whom God has sent because, just as in Isaiah's time, people have failed to recognise their Lord and provider. God's people, all of them, have gone astray. As Saint Paul was to put it: 'All have sinned and fall short of the glory of God' (Rom 3:23). God's answer to this universal human tragedy is to send his son, the infant in the manger, who will grow up to proclaim, 'The Son of Man came to seek out and to save the lost' (Lk 19:10).

The God who sends his son Jesus is a God forsaken: forsaken and forgotten by his people. But God will not allow his people to be godforsaken. Jesus is the final proof that God will not turn his back on those who turn their backs on him. In theological terms, turning away from God is always a kind of idolatry, since to turn away from God is to turn towards something else, to put something else in God's place, to make a god of what is not God. Some words God spoke through the prophet Jeremiah clearly convey the essence of idolatry: 'My people have committed two evils: they have forsaken me, the fountain of living water, and dug out cisterns for themselves, cracked cisterns that can hold no water' (Jer 2:13). The definitive and perfect answer to this crisis is found in the words Jesus spoke to the Samaritan woman at the well: 'Everyone who drinks of this water will be thirsty again, but those who drink of the water that I will give them will never be thirsty. The water that I will give will become in them a spring of water gushing up to eternal life' (Jn 4:13-14). In Jesus, we see that it is God, not human stupidity, wilfulness, forgetfulness or neglect, that has the upper hand.

And so to the lamb, the least of the creatures in the crib, and the most powerfully symbolic of all. Denise Levertov, in her poem 'Mass for the Day of St Thomas Didymus', captures the strange and paradoxical quality of the lamb-symbolism of the New Testament:

> Given that lambs
> are infant sheep, that sheep
> are afraid and foolish, and lack
> the means of self-protection, having
> neither rage nor claws,
> venom nor cunning,
> what then
> is this 'Lamb of God'?

The inclusion of lambs in our cribs, even though they are not mentioned in the Gospel accounts of the birth of Jesus, reminds us that Jesus is the Lamb of God. The lambs are not, therefore, a nod in the direction of sentimentality, or something to intrigue and entertain the youngest visitors to the crib. Like the ox and the ass, they are profoundly biblical, and they too can serve as interpreters of the child in the crib. Whereas the ox and ass remind us of why Jesus has come – because God's people have strayed – the lamb can remind us of how Jesus will remedy this state of affairs: Jesus is 'the Lamb of God who takes away the sin of the world' (Jn 1:29). In order to do this, to restore the relationship between God and his people, Jesus will use 'Neither rage nor claws, venom nor cunning', but only love. He will take away the sins of the world by taking them upon himself.

The presence of lambs in our crib can point to the fact that Jesus overcomes, not by force or resistance, but by the kind of strong, gentle love that bears the name of sacrifice. Up to the time of Jesus, animals were offered in the Temple in Jerusalem as a sacrifice for sin, and it has been suggested that the shepherds to whom the angel announced the birth of Jesus were tending the very creatures that were destined for the Temple sacrifice; but whatever the truth of that suggestion, only one Lamb could effectively deal with the sins of the world: the child in the manger at Bethlehem. Jesus, the Lamb of God, is the new Passover lamb: he offers himself as food at the Passover meal (Mk 14:12-25); he is the lamb that is sacrificed (1 Cor 5:7); he is the sacrificial victim about whom the scriptures give the instruction, 'You shall not break any of its bones' (Ex 12:46; Jn 19:31-36). In the crib, the angels proclaim aloud that the newborn child is our Saviour; the lamb, wordlessly, proclaims the kind of Saviour he is.

'The manger is situated on Golgotha, and the cross has already been raised in Bethlehem.' These words were written by Dag Hammarskjöld in his spiritual journal, *Markings*, on Christmas Eve 1960. They point to the fact that crib and cross are inseparable elements of a single mystery, a single rescue-plan for humanity. The wood of the manger anticipates the wood of the cross; the child who now lies helpless in the manger will hang helplessly on the cross. The manger thus provides a final, silent reminder of the intimate connection between Christmas and Easter. It is on the cross that Jesus gives himself to men and women as the 'Bread of life' (Jn 6:35). On Calvary, Jesus carries out what his words at the last supper had anticipated: 'This is my body, which is given for you ... this cup that is poured out for you is the new covenant in my blood' (Lk 22:19-20). But now, the one who is to offer himself as food for humanity lies in a feeding trough.

The crib scene, for all its innocent charm, anticipates what Jesus will do and suffer. Far from being a flight from the harshness of reality, the crib invites us to reflect on the reality of sin, and to contemplate the Lord's unfathomably generous self-offering. As Hammarskjöld suggested, Calvary began at the manger, and as we noted earlier, the shadow of the cross falls across the crib. None of this takes from the joy of Christ's birthday; on the contrary, it means that those who live in the shadow of the cross can share fully in the hope we celebrate at Christmas.

The early Christians interpreted the events of Christ's life by carefully reading their Bible. Jesus himself set the precedent for such reading: during his walk with two disciples on the road to Emmaus, 'Beginning with Moses and all the prophets, he interpreted to them the things about himself in all the scriptures' (Lk 24:27). Jesus is understood in the light of the Old Testament; and just as surely, for Christians, the Old Testament is fully illuminated by the light of Christ. One of the most important Old Testament texts for our understanding of Christ's passion is found in Isaiah, where we read: 'All we like sheep have gone astray; we have all turned to our own way, and the Lord has laid on him the iniquity of us all. He was oppressed, and he was afflicted, yet he did not open his mouth; like a lamb that is led to the slaughter, and like a sheep that before its shearers is silent, so he did not open his mouth' (Isa 53:6-7). The child in the manger is the lamb of God who, on Calvary, bears and takes away the sin of the world; he is also the Good Shepherd (Jn 10:11), and he is the victorious, heavenly King: 'The lamb at the centre of the throne will be their shepherd, and he will guide them to springs of the water of life, and God will wipe away every tear from their eyes' (Rev 7:17). The followers of the Lamb are people of realism and gratitude: they know that while they have strayed, they have also been found and are now being guided by the Good Shepherd, who has laid down his life for his sheep.

Points to ponder

+ We, God's straying but beloved children, are sometimes God-forsaking, but never godforsaken: 'If we are faithless, he remains faithful' (2 Tim 2:13). Our infidelities do not have the last word; the last word belongs to God, and his name is Jesus. Human waywardness is no abstraction: its consequences are concrete and destructive. Sinful, selfish and thoughtless behaviour leaves real suffering in its wake, so much so that we can speak of a record of sin. The letter to the Colossians uses a lovely image to describe how Christ dealt with human sinfulness and its consequences: in Christ, God was 'Erasing the record that stood against us with its legal demands. He set this aside, nailing it to the cross' (Col 2:14). Many people feel burdened by their past, by their sins and misjudgements, by the harsh judgements of others; but far from being an obstacle, our burdens are an invitation to come to the Lord, to pause trustfully before the child in the manger. The further we may feel from Christ, the more we may be able to sense the appeal of the Christ-child, who does not keep an account of sins, but whose currency is mercy and compassion. In the gentleness of the infant, we can encounter the risen Lord and hear his gentle invitation.

+ If the crib were a church, we would have to describe it as a 'broad church'. It includes the great and the humble, the wise and the simple, the distinguished and the unlettered. Furthermore, the Gospel accounts of the first Christmas are filled with references to governance and governors, journeys and sojourners, gifts and gift-bearers. Our reflections have shown that life is present here in all its abundant variety and complexity, and it is in the variety and complexity of life that God works. Something of God is manifested in nature, animals, stars, light and darkness, the timber of a feeding trough. In theological language, this hands-on characteristic of God's presence and action is referred to as 'sacramentality'. Our God is not an abstraction, a vague principle, but a loving father who ceaselessly works in concrete reality, in 'things' like water, bread and wine. As we approach the crib at Christmas, we can do so in the confidence that the God who became utterly present at the edge of a small town just beyond the outskirts of Jerusalem is present in the backwaters and cul-de-sacs of our own lives. The ordinariness of life, its 'bread and water', and life's sufferings, the things which crush us as grapes are crushed in the production of wine, are not places from which God is absent, but the very arena in which he acts.

+ The child in the crib has changed reality for all of humanity, but his love is not for humanity in the abstract. Christ's love is for each and every person; the Lamb of God, who takes away the sin of the world, loves each individual with a personal, customised, tailor-made love. It is for this reason that we can make our own the words of the Psalmist, 'The Lord is my shepherd, I shall not want' (Ps 23:1). Our hope is in Christ, and it is this hope that allows us to say with confidence, 'Surely goodness and mercy shall follow me all the days of my life, and I shall dwell in the house of the Lord my whole life long' (Ps 23:6).